I0119048

Lyman Haynes Low

Catalogue of the extensive and valuable collection of copper coins and tokens

Lyman Haynes Low

Catalogue of the extensive and valuable collection of copper coins and tokens

ISBN/EAN: 9783741130557

Manufactured in Europe, USA, Canada, Australia, Japa

Cover: Foto ©Andreas Hilbeck / pixelio.de

Manufactured and distributed by brebook publishing software
(www.brebook.com)

Lyman Haynes Low

Catalogue of the extensive and valuable collection of copper coins and tokens

PART I.

CATALOGUE

OF THE

EXTENSIVE AND VALUABLE COLLECTION

OF

COPPER COINS *AND* TOKENS,

THE PROPERTY OF

COLONEL WALTER CUTTING,

OF PITTSFIELD, MASSACHUSETTS,

CONSISTING IN PART OF CANADA, WITH MANY OF ITS NOTED RARITIES, INCLUDING THE

PATTERN SET OF THE BOUT DE L'ISLE TOKENS,

UNITED STATES, COLONIALS, HARD TIMES TOKENS, WEST INDIA ISLANDS,
AMONG WHICH ARE THE VERY RARE

SOMMER ISLANDS SIXPENCE AND SHILLING,

MEXICO, SOUTH AMERICA AND GREAT BRITAIN,

ENGLISH TOKENS AS DESCRIBED BY CONDER,

WITH A MAGNIFICENT ARRAY OF

SIEGE AND NECESSITY PIECES, CHIEFLY IN SILVER.

Which will be Sold by Public Auction at

The Rooms of the COLLECTORS' CLUB, 351 Fourth Ave., New York,

HENRY C. MERRY, Auctioneer,

MONDAY AND TUESDAY, MAY 23 and 24, 1898,

AT TWO O'CLOCK EACH DAY.

The Coins will be on Exhibition from 9.30 A. M., to 1 P. M.

CATALOGUED BY
LYMAN H. LOW,
UNITED CHARITIES BUILDING, FOURTH AVENUE AND 22d STREET,
NEW YORK, N. Y.

COINS AND MEDALS

(The closing number or that following name of coin)

In this Catalogue, is given in Millimeters.

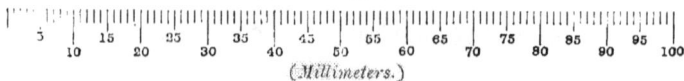

(*Millimeters.*)

ABBREVIATIONS USED.

abt.	about.	*l.*	left.	sep.	separate. / separating.
Æ	Copper.	Lib.	Liberty.		
ÆR	Silver.	mil.	military.	std.	seated.
bet.	between.	*m. m.*	mint mark.	setd.	
bril.	brilliant.	mon.	monogram.	shld.	shield.
bzd.	bronzed.	mtd.	mounted.	sim.	similar.
Ctvs.	Centavos.	n. d.	no date.	sq.	square.
C.S.	Counterstamped.	O.	Obverse.	stdg.	standing.
Cwn.	Crown.	*Obv.*		supl.	supplement.
cwnd.	crowned.	oct.	octagonal.	sup.	supported.
dbl.	double.	octag.		suptd.	
dif.	different.	orig.	original.	Trans.	Translation.
do.	ditto.	pc.	piece.	unc.	uncirculated.
Ex.	Exergue.	pf.	proof.	v.	very.
ex.	extra.	*r.*	right.	var.	variety. / varieties.
gd.	good.	℞	Reverse.		
hd.	head.	*Rev.*		W.m.	White metal.
imp.	Imperial.	*Res.*	restrike.	wrth.	wreath.
Ins.	inscription.	Rl.	Reals.		
		Rls.			

U. S. Mints are designated as follows: C., Charlotte; C. C., Carson City; D., Dahlonega; O., New Orleans; S., San Francisco; without letter, Philadelphia.

*** All manner of copies, alterations and other imposi-tions are excluded from my sales.

*** There are no duplicates in any lot unless so men-tioned specially.

Copies of this Catalogue with Three Plates, giving prices realized, neatly executed in red ink, $1.00.

☞ INSTRUCTIONS TO BIDDERS.

Coins and medals are sold at so much per piece, U. S. proof sets excepted. You cannot bid for one piece in a lot. If a lot contains ten pieces, and you desire to offer $2 for it, make your bid 20c. The auctioneer will accept an advance of 1 cent up to 50c., then 5c. up to $2.50, when 10c. is the limit, up to $10, and thereafter not less than 25c. Hence any bid up to 50c. can be entertained, but after that the bid must be 55c., 60c., and so on. Such offers as 53c., $1.01, and all intermediate figures are unavailable.

INTRODUCTORY NOTE.

THE Copper Coins grouped and briefly described in the
following pages, comprise the most extensive and important collection which in my long experience, I have
ever before catalogued for public sale. The work of arranging
has been productive of more than usual interest, from the fact
of my having shared with the owner the pleasure of gathering
together much of the cabinet, the foundation of which was laid
about eighteen years ago.

It would be needless repetition to note particular pieces, or
comment in detail upon any of the many noteworthy series. It
is enough to say that no such cabinet of ENGLISH TOKENS as
described by Conder, has ever before been dispersed, if indeed
any such has ever been gathered in this country. These little
pieces have much historical and archæological value, from the
views they bear, and heralds and genealogists also prize them
highly. There will be found, also, many of the earlier Tokens
described by Boyne, in which some very curious pieces are in-
cluded. Several of the most remarkable of the later Tokens have
been selected for illustration. The plates will be found at the
close of the Catalogue, and while they give as fair a representa-
tion as could be expected from phototypes from the same nega-
tive, of pieces varying in color, thickness, etc., there is no possi-

bility of flattery, and an imperfect light or faulty development
may do injustice, as is particularly the case in the figure of No.
223 (Cent of 1799), Plate 1.

With those just mentioned will be found a large number of
pieces from Scandinavia, the Low Countries, France, Spain, and
Portugal, and a very large and attractive line of *Russian Coins
and Patterns*, and at the close, many rare Siege and Necessity
pieces in Silver and Copper. The Catalogue tells the story, and
those interested and familiar with the science, will recognize the
extent, rarity and high state of preservation recorded in its pages.

It has been found expedient to divide the sale, in consequence
of which Part II will be offered early in the autumn, and will con-
tain some equally important series of the remainder of the modern
coinages of the world.

In addition to calling attention to my invariable rule of rigidly
excluding counterfeits and all impositions from my sales, I think
it opportune to state here that collectors will find the conditions
of the coins, etc., to correspond exactly with catalogue represen-
tation — attention being invariably called to restrikes and pieces
which are holed, scoured, or cleaned, or have loops removed — in
accordance with a practice I have always observed, as all pur-
chasers at my sales can readily testify.

L. H. L.

April 15th, 1898.

CATALOGUE.

BRITISH NORTH AMERICA.

1.30   1   **Newfoundland.** 1860 Fishery rights for Newfoundland. V. fine, rare.   1

11   2   Cents. 1865, '72, '73, '76 Fine to unc.; 2 of last.   4

7   3   Rutherford, St. John's. 1841 and n.d. Harbour Grace, 1846. Var. of obv.; the last 2 by *Robert Heaton.* Good to v. fine.   4

CANADA IN GENERAL.

50   4   1721, '22 Colonies Francoises. Both H. mint. Poor and good.   2

2.70   5   1751 Louis XV, Jeton. Bust (and all have, to include lot 12, excepting 7). ℞ Sub omni sidere crescunt. Indian stdg. *Ex.* Col · Franc · de · | l'Am. *Restrike.* V. fine. 29. Betts, 385.   1

3.45   6   1752 Jeton. Utrique facit commercia mundo. Mercury soaring *l. Res.* Perfect. 30. B. 386.   1

3.25   7   1752 Jeton. Protegit et pascit. Arms of the West India Co., supt. ℞ As last. *Res.* V. fine. 29. B. 387.   1

3.35   8   1753 Jeton. Satis unus utrique. Two hemispheres. *Res.* V. fine. 29½. B. 388.   1

3.60   9   1754 Jeton. Non inferiora metallis. Beaver and plants. *Res.* V. fine. 29. B. 389.   1

3.00   10   1755 Jeton. Non vilius aureo. A galley *l. Res.* V. fine. 29. B. 390.   1

11.50   11   1756 Jeton. Sedem non animum mutant. Bees swarming from old to new hive. Original, unc., red. Very rare. 29. B. 393.   1

11,00 **12** 1758 Jeton. Eadem trans æquora virtus. Birds flying above
sea. *Res.* V. fine. 29. B. 395.   1

。 **13** 1767 Colonies Francoises, with and without CS. R. F. Sous.
Good.   2

. , **14** 1781 No. Am. Token. V. fair. 1805 Field-Marshal Wellington Halfp. *Fine.* Also, Penny with same Hibernia, rev.
type. Breton, 975. Good.   3

₂ 00 **15** 1810 Windmill bet. branches. ℞ NO CREDIT; exterior and interior view of bldg. Halfp. V. fair.   1

This piece came from the Sandham sale, 1884, lot 67, where it brought $2.00. I am
hardly prepared to assert that it ever homed in Canada, but wherever it may have strayed
from, I have yet to see its duplicate.

2,60 **16** 1811 "Vexator Canadiensis" and "Canadinsis." Halfpennies.
V.-fair, quite as good as usual; rare in any condition.   2

40 **17** 1811 Vincit amor patriæ. Bust *r.* Halfpennies. Varieties;
2 very choice.   3

1.30 **18** 1812 *R H* ℞ Ship sailing *l.* FARTHING TOKEN 1814; do.
Halfp., thick and thin planchet (plain and engrailed edge);
also, Penny. A fine, complete and *rare* set.   4

7 5 **19** 1812 Bust *r.*, head laur. within closed wreath. ℞ Commerce
setd *l.* Ex. date. Halfp., 2 var., and Penny. Fine.   3

2 5 **20** 1812 Sim. date on obv. Another dated on both sides. Good.   2

21 1812 Halfpennies of sim. design to 19 (3 var.), with 5 others
in brass, slightly varying. Good to fine.   8

,5 **22** 1812 Others modelled after the two preceding, but indifferently
executed. Good. Brass.   8

14 **23** 1812 Commerce setd *l.* Ex. date. ℞ Ship. 2 var. 1815, same
type, edge milled. Halfpennies. Fine.   3

? 9 **24** 1812 Trade & Nav. Commerce setd *l.* ℞ Pure copper, etc.;
value in field. Halfp. 1813 Halfp. and Penny (2 var. of
latter). V. good to fine, partly bright.   4

4 ,0 **25** 1813 Field-Marshal Wellington. Halfp.; also Penny with Vimiera, Talavera, etc. Both have bust *l.* V. good, rare.   2

- - **26** 1813 Trade & Nav. Ship *l.* ℞ Pure copper, etc. Obv. and
rev. from dies varying (2). Marquis Wellington. Bust *r.*
Halfpennies. Wellington & Erin go bragh. ℞ E. Stephens
— Dublin (2). Obv. dies differ. Pennies. V. good.   5

r. , **27** 1813 ONE PENNY TOKEN. Ship *r.* ℞ ONE | PENNY | TOKEN
within closed wrth. Fine. Extremely rare.   1

3 C **28** 1813 HALFPENNY above lion on line *l.* (3) ; another dated 1814
(scarce). Fine to unc. ; partly bright.   4

Originally for Walthamstowe.

/ **29** 1813 Halfpenny Token. Eagle. ℞ Commerce setd *l.* 2 var. ;
1814, 4 var. ; 1815, 2 var. The differences are in rev. dies.
Good to fine.   8

2,0 **30** 1814 "Half Penny Token." Bust *r.* ℞ For the convenience
of Trade. Ship *r.* Fine, rare.   1

2 0 **31** 1814 Wellington — Halfpenny Token. 3 var. Great Britain.
Bust. ℞ Commerce. 3 var. Trade & Nav. Penny, Com-
merce setd *l.* Fair to v. good.   7

/ 2 **32** 1815 Halfpenny Token. Bust *r.* ℞ Genuine British Copper.
Britannia setd *l.* (2 var.) Sim. ℞ Success to Nav. etc.
Ship *r.* (3 var., 1 holed). Good to v. fine. (Halfpenny) To-
ken. Bust *r.* Cwnd harp within wrth. Poor but rare.   6

30 **33** 1815 Genuine British Copper. Bust *r.* Wellington | Waterloo.
℞ Ship. "Ships Colonies and Commerce." ℞ One | Half-
penny | Token Another, For | publick | accommodation.
Brass (both are also credited to Isle of Man.) 1816 Waterloo
Halfpenny. Fair to fine ; scarce lot.   5

/. **34** 1816 Wellington & Erin go bragh. Bust *l.* by *I. Parkes* (of
Dublin). ℞ Edwd. Stephens. Var. of obv. and rev. Pen-
nies. Good and fine.   2

/ **35** 1820 Bust *l.* ℞ Harp, date below. Varieties ; 2 struck without a collar. Halfpennies. Good to fine. Brass, 10. Æ, 1.   11

'/ 4 **36** 1820 Bust *r.* ℞ Commerce setd *l.* Trade and Nav. Ship.
·Hibernicus (2 var.) 1825 To Facilitate Trade (2 var.) Good
to v. fine and choice.   6

/.bu **36a** 1825 Bust *l.* Same as on British Colonies, with branch at
sides added. ℞ Edward Barnsley — Contractor. 3 Pence.
Fine. Brass.   1

Placed here only for its similarity to piece referred to.

4/,/ **37** 1826 GEORGIUS IV D : G : RE(X :) Head *l.* Patterned after the
rare Colonial issues of 1823. ℞ BRITANNIA. Female setd
l. on union-jack, holds trident and shamrock. Edge plain.
Penny. Very good. Bold and rather rude work. Rare.   1

4,35 **38** 1828 COMMERCE. Ship *l.* ℞ ONE : FARTHING — TOKEN : Date
in field. Fine, very rare.   1

6

BRITISH NORTH AMERICA.

39 1830 (and '41) Canada Halfp. 1838 Trade & Nav. Penny.
1858, '59, '76, '81 Victoria Cents. Good to unc. 7

40 1858 Ship *r*. Type of the usual S. C. & C. pcs., though much
better executed. ℞ 1858. Very fine, extremely rare; said
to have been issued by a Newfoundland merchant. 1

Halfpennies, without date.

41 Bust *r*. (from 3 dies); *revs.*, Ships | Colonies | & | Commerce
(3) and Commercial | Change. Fair to fine. 4

42 Brutus (2), Field-Marshal Wellington (2), Victoria nobis est,
Mercury (2). Good to v. fine. 7

43 Bust *r*. Gloriuvs. The Blacksmith's Halfp. and 2 others, differing, with blank revs. Bust *l*.; revs., Harp and setd figure.
Poor to good, 1 holed. 3 are really rare. 8

44 The Blacksmith's obv. ℞ ISEINGTON — TAVERN and 12 others
on planchets split from Peck's Troy card, 1 holed. All very
rare. 3

45 Man with shamrock. No Labour No Bread (2 var.) For Public Accommodation, Ship, 2 var. of rev. 9 cards displayed.
Good to fine. 6

45a Napoleon. Head *l*., laur. ℞ C'EST DU CUIVRE. Ship with
British flag sailing *r*. Halfpenny and Farthing size, the latter signed by *J. Davis*. (Birm.) Fine and very rare, especially the smaller one. Brass. 2

I am not aware that the history of these two pieces has ever been made public, but
with the many promiscuous tokens found in Canada up to the introduction of the Cent
in 1858, these may have found companionship. Napoleon's memory, among the French
Canadians, has ever been treasured; what stronger attest could there be than the large
number of given names, in his honor, found among them?

46 SHIPS | COLONIES | & | COMMERCE. *Believed* to be all different,
1 with obv. impression only; also "drooping" and American
flag (2, one with W. & B. N. Y.) Good to fine. 24

47 Another with W. & B. N. Y. beneath water line. Unc., partly
bright. Very rare. 1

48 A ship *r*. ℞ Halfpenny Token. Commerce setd *l*. Breton,
1005. Good, rare. 1

49 Wellington. Mil. bust *l*. ℞ Names and dates of battles.
Fine, 6 (1 holed). Also, a Communion Token, oblong, lead.
LeR. 907. 7

4.00 **50** VIMIERA TALAVERA. etc. Bust *l.* ℟ COSSACK — PENNY TOKEN
A Cossack mtd *r.* Unc., partly bright, very rare.   1

MAGDALEN ISLAND.

1.3 **51** 1815 Magdalen Island Token. A seal *r.* ℟ A dried codfish.
Fine, a few nicks.   1

PRINCE EDWARD ISLAND.

16.25 **52** 1840 Sheaf of wheat and sickle. ℟ COMMERCE & TRADE. A
plow *l.* Fair, very rare.   1

8 **53** 1855 Fisheries and Agriculture, 3 var. Prince Edward and
Edward's, 5 var. 1857 Edward, 6 var. Fine to unc.   14

11 **54** 1871 Victoria Cent, unc., red ; also Steamship Token, Plow
and Codfish, 3 var., and Communion Token of St. John
Parish in lead. Good to fine.   6

.5 **55** Communion Tokens, St. John Parish. Oval. LeR. 358, 359.
V. good, rare ; lead.   2

NOVA SCOTIA.

1/ **56** 1823 (2 var.), '24 (2 var.), '32 (5 var.), '40, '43 Halfpennies.
Bust. ℟ Thistle. Fair to fine.   11

1.30 **57** 1824 Bust *l.* ℟ ONE PENNY TOKEN Thistle. V. fine, medium
olive. Rare when so choice.   1

C **58** Other Pennies. 1824 (var. of last), 1832 (5 var.), '40, '43. Fair
to very good.   8

9 **59** 1856 Victoria. Thistle Halfp. and Penny. 1861 Half Cent
and Cent. 1864 Do. do. All uncirculated ; most are red.
Very desirable.   6

30 **60** 1862 Cent, scarce. Halifax Tokens : Barry, Black's, 1816.
Keg, shovel, spade, scythe, etc. (2 var.) ; Blakley. Good to
v. fine ; most of last.   5

2.5 **61** 1814 Broke, Carritt & Alport, Hosterman & Etter (also 1815) ;
1815 Starr & Shannon, Com'l Ch'ge, White, Halifax, with 2
var. of obv., and undated Ferry Token ; also J. Brown. Good
to v. fine.   11

2.10 **62** W. L. White's — Halifax House, Halifax. ONE | FARTHING
Rare.   1

.55 **63** Sᵀ· MATHEW'S | CHURCH | HALIFAX N. S. Oblong octagon Com-
munion Token. LeR. 463. Lead. V. fine. Robert Purves,
Wallace. V. good.   2

6,25 **64** NOVA SCOTIA AND NEW BRUNSWICK — SUCCESS A ship *r*. ℟
HALFPENNY TOKEN. Commerce setd *l*. Uncirculated ; partly
bright. A rare gem.   1

NEW BRUNSWICK.

/* **65** St. John Halfp. Victoria, 1843 ½ and 1 Penny. 1854 Do. do.
1861 ½ Cent (good, rare) and Cent. 1864 Cent. D(umfries)
K(irk) | 1833 Communion Token (lead). Mostly v. fine.   9

11,00 **66** F. MᶜDERMOTT . | IMPORTER | OF ENGLISH, | FRENCH & GERMAN
| FANCY GOODS | KING Sᵀ. | Sᴺᵀ JOHN. N. B. ℟ DEPOSITORY
OF ARTS. Arms. V. fine ; slightest signs of circulation. V.
rare.   1

PROVINCE OF QUEBEC.

25.00 **67** Hunterstown. 1852 A pine cone within wrth. ℟ PAYABLE .
IN . GOODS . A 5-ptd star within wrth. Current for a Halfp.
Very fair ; extremely rare.   1

I believe but four examples of this token are known.

30 **68** Montreal. 1816 Ship Halfp. 1837 B'k of Montreal Halfp.
and Penny ; Banque du Peuple Halfp. ; City Bank Halfp.
and Penny. All with Habitant on obv. Fine to unc.   6

3,75 **69** 1837 TH: & W.ᴹ· MOLSON. etc. BREWERS | DISTILLERS | .. & . & . & ..
A cask, UN — SOU Fine, scarce.   1

30,25 **70** 1838 BANK OF MONTREAL. Front and side view of building.
Tree *r*. before fence, with 5 pales *r*., 3 *l*. Half Penny. Very
fine, strong impression, and not in concave style, as the piece
is usually found. Very rare.   1

32,50 **71** 1838 Penny. Type as last. " Bank of Montreal " on label, is
in relief on this and the preceding ; the following have it
incuse. Extremely fine and deep impression ; slightest indi-
cation of circulation. Extremely rare.   1

17,00 **72** 1839 Half Penny. Type of two preceding. Extremely fine ;
rare.   1

9,25 **73** 1839 Another from same dies as last. Very good ; rare.   1

33,00 **74** 1839 Penny of same type. Very fine ; extremely rare.   1

110 **75** 1842 Halfp. and Penny. 1844 Halfp. Front view of Bank of
Montreal (2), v. fine and partly bright. 1867 Devins & Bolton's card, with obv. type of Canadian Cent. Unc., red.   4

75a 1887 German Choral Society. Tokens for 5 Cents. Obv. with head of Wilhelm (3 types), Fred. III, Leo XIII. Æ, proofs.   5

76 Bout de l'Isle Tokens. *All very rare.* CHEVAL. ℞ DE L'ISLE | DE MONTREAL. | A REPENTIGUY | ON | LACHESNAYE Fine.   1

77 — PERSONNE ℞ From same die as last. Fine.   1

78 — Obv. as last. ℞ DE REPENTIGUY | A | L'ISLE DE | MONTREAL | .. * .. | ON LACHESNAYE. Unc., partly bright.   1

Here are a high state of preservation and extreme rarity combined together, something very unusual.

79 — A pattern set of Bout de l'Isle Tokens. ON | REPENTIGUY, A | REPENTIGUY, and DE | REPENTIGUY, each with reverses. CALECHE, CHARETTE, CHEVAL and PERSONNE. Breton, 546 to 558. Bronzed proofs.   12

This set, long in obscurity, first publicly made its appearance at a London sale in July, 1890, where it was noted most unostentatiously, with many tokens of the 18th century in the same lot. Its origin and striking, unquestionably, must be credited to the same period as the preceding. I have yet to learn of another set or a single specimen belonging to it, and I have come to regard it as unique, therefore of the highest rarity, besides being endowed with historic interest. See my letter regarding this set, written Oct. 19th, 1893, published in Mr. Breton's " Illustrated History of Coins and Tokens relating to Canada."

80 T. S. Brown & Co., 2 var. ; E. A. Cardinal (2 types, brass) ; Devins & Bolton, punched (2, one on Deanston — Cotton Mill Token) ; Dr. LeRoux, 2 types (1 in brass). Good to fine.   8

81 Lymburner & Brother, Gold and Silver Platers, Æ and lead ; M. E. Lymburner, Æ (*very* rare) and Æ. Unc. ; none common.   4

82 MONTREAL & LACHINE — Railroad Company. A locomotive *l.* Original hole in centre. Fine, scarce.   1

82a Maysenholder & Bohle — Gold Smiths. Established 1849. ℞ MONT . REAL etc. Uncirculated, rare.   1

83 FRANCIS MULLINS & SON etc. Commerce — Token. Ship *r.* Fine. Æ and brass, the latter rare.   2

84 R · W · OWEN. | MONTREAL | ROPERY within circle formed by two strands of rope twisted. ℞ A ship *r.* Beaded borders, edge diagonally milled. Halfpenny. One of the most celebrated rarities of the series, and in fine condition. Few have so high a record of value.   1

85 R. Sharpley, Jeweller & Watchmaker. Unc. (brass). J^h. Roy. 2 maple leaves crossed. V. good ; both scarce.   2

/ 86 Sou Tokens. Bank of Montreal, Banque du Peuple, Bank To-
      ken and Token — Montreal. LeR. 508, 509 (2 sizes), 518 to
      521 ? 522 ? 523 ? 525, 536, 538 to 547 (2 metals of last), 550,
      551, 552, 554, 556, 557, 558 ? 560, 561, 563, 564, 568, 569,
      570, 571 ? 574. Numbered in separate envelopes. Many fine.   39

  87 Sou. Very distinct and superior in character of workmanship,
      in planchet, and in striking, from others of the series. LeR.
      553. Very fine and very rare. Brass.   1

  88 Another from dies discovered about 1860 ; none found in cir-
      culation. One of about 20 struck at the instigation of the
      Montreal Numismatic Society. Not a perfect impression (I
      have never seen one that was). LeR. 549. Very rare.   1

  89 Another as last, struck on a square planchet, 33 x 33 ; sim. con-
      dition, rarer than the preceding.   1

  90 St. Andrew's and St. Paul's (1833) Church, Montreal. Com-
      munion Tokens. Fine, rare. Lead.   2

  91 **Quebec.** 1837 Quebec Bank, Halfp. and Penny. 1852 Do.
      do., H. Gagnon & Cie ; J. Shaw ; Three Rivers, R. W. Wil-
      liams. Fine to unc.   7

  92 A very crude Penny, without date, designed after the Habitant
      type, with large and indistinguishable (or meaningless) letters
      or characters. The very worst example of die engraving I
      have seen.   1

ONTARIO.

  93 Sloop Halfpennies. *Rev.*, Com'l Change. 1815 Indian and
      his dog. 1821 Spade and shovel crossed, 3 var. 1823 Plow,
      2 var. 1833 Plow. Brock monument, 1816, 4 var. Good
      to fine.   11

  94 Success to the Commerce, etc. Ship *r.* ℞ Ins. in 9 lines,
      ending 1812. Another with same obverse. ℞ Success to
      Commerce, etc. 1816 in field. Rare, good.   2

  95 1821 Cask ins. UPPER | CANADA ℞ Sloop. Good, rare. 1833
      Com'l Ch'ge ; spade and shovel, vise, scythe, etc. Fine,
      scarce.   2

  96 Bank of Upper Canada. 1850, '52, '54, '57 Halfp. and Penny
      of each date. Good to unc. 4 of last.   8

  97 Lesslie & Sons Halfpenny, 3 var. Province of Upper Canada
      Halfp. Good to fine.   4

11.75 98 LESSLIE & SONS . TORONTO & DUNDAS — 1822 Justice stdg. ℞
Plow. Very fine ; difficult to equal, few excel. Rare. 1

2.0 99 HAMILTON | RETAILERS | TOKEN ℞ ONE FARTHING | 1814. 1
Not Hamilton, Ontario.

35 100 Communion Tokens. Baltimore, 1855 ; Centreville (LeR.
713) ; Grafton, 1844 ; Orillia, 1855 ; Stratford, 1858 ; Toronto, 1852, and LeR. 908. Fine, rare. Lead. 7

NORTH-WEST.

17.00 101 TOKEN — 1820 Bust *r.* ℞ NORTH WEST — (Company). Beaver *r.* Very fair ; holed, as I believe all are. V. rare. 28½. 1

3 102 Duplicate Canadas. Halfpennies, 1781 to 1886 (including 2
Farthings) and others without date. A few poor, 1 holed,
but mostly very good. 85

55 103 — Pennies, 1805-57, including the very rare 1813 Ship Token
(same as lot 27), in fine condition ; Cossack, very fair, and
others. Poor (3) to fine. 12

UNITED STATES.

3.00 104 Colonial and Continental. Jas. II. 1685-88, $\frac{1}{24}$ Real.
The king mtd *r.* ℞ Four shlds of British arms chained in
cross form. Unc. Tin. 28. 1

60 105 (1694) Elephant *l.*, same as New England and Carolina piece.
℞ God Preserve London. Scratched, otherwise good. B.
81. 1

30 106 1722 Rosa-Americana Halfp. and Penny. Rose uncrowned.
UTILE and VTILE Poor to good. 3

26 107 1723 Penny and Twopence. Rose crowned. Barely fair. 2

10 108 Others with dates indistinguishable. Rose crowned. Penny
(1), Twopence (3). 4

25.5 109 Woods' Series. 1722 George I. Head *r.* ℞ HIBERNIÆ ·
Hibernia setd before column of rocks, holding harp. Halfpenny. Nearly fine ; very rare. 1

50 110 1722 Harp before setd figure, die varieties of obv. and rev.
Another of same date, with harp behind figure. Good to
fine ; none common. 4

111 1723 Harp behind figure. Farthing and Halfp. 1724 Halfp.
V. good to fine. 3

112   1723 Farthings (3), Halfpennies (6), from dies differing, and
unlike the preceding. Good to fine.   9

113   1722 Others still varying. Far. (2), Halfp. (6). 1724 Halfp.
(2). Mostly v. good.   10

114   1766 Bust of Wm. Pitt. ℞ AMERICA. Ship. 1767 Col.
Francoises. CS. R. F. 1781 No. American Token. Good.   3

115   1776 CONTINENTAL CURRENCY. A sun-dial, FUGIO etc. ℞
Names of States on 13 links united in chain encircling
AMERICAN CONGRESS . WE | ARE | ONE V. fine. Rare. Tin. 39.   1

115a Another from same dies. T. W. punched on obv. and name
ending in PPING CS. on rev. Very fair.   1

116   1783 Washington Cents. "Unity" "United States" togated
and military bust ; also dbl-headed Cent, n.d. Good and
very good.   4

117   1783 Nova "Constelatio" and Constellatio. Large and small
U·S and differing wreaths. Very good.   2

118   1785 Nova "Constelatio" and Constellatio. 3 varieties of
latter. Fair, good and nearly fine (2 of last).   4

119   1787 Immunis Columbia. Female setd on globe holds flag
and scales. ℞ E Pluribus Unum. Eagle. V. good, rare.   1

120   1787 Fugio or Franklin Cents. Club rays and "States United" and "United States." Good to fine.   3

121   1787 Fugios from varying dies, and different from preceding.   5

122   1789 GEO. WASHINGTON etc. Bust *l.* ℞ General | of the |
American Armies | etc. Obv. fair, rev. very poor, holed.
Rare.   1

123   1791 Washington President Bust *l.* ℞ ONE CENT above
large eagle. V. good, rare.   1

124   George Washington. Bust *l.* ℞ Liberty and Security. Penny.
V. good.   1

125   George Washington. Bust *r.* ℞ Success to the United
States. Fine, scarce. Size 20 and 25.   2

125a Bar Cent, U S A linked. ℞ 13 parallel bars. From circulation. Good, rare.   1

THE COINAGE OF THE STATES.

126   **Vermont.** (1785) VERMON AUCTORI Bust *r.* ℞ IMMUNE
COLUMBIA Female setd *r.* Planchet too small to show
date. Good, rare.   1

1,10 **127** 1785 Vermonts and Vermontis. Sun rising from behind hills, plow below. V. fair. 2

128 1786 Cents of similar type, with Vermontensium. Slight varieties. Poor and good. 2

129 1786 Vermon Auctori. Mailed busts *l.* (2), and Auctori : Vermon : Baby head *r.* Others of 1787 (1), 1788 (3). Mostly good. 7

1,5 **130** 1787 and '88. Both fine. 2

131 1788 Varieties of preceding, including 2 with GEORGIVS . III . REX . on obverse. Poor to good. 9

6 **132 Massachusetts.** 1787 Half Cent and Cent. Eagle. ℞ COMMON WEALTH Indian stdg. V. good. 2

0 **133** 1788 Half Cent and Cent. Very good ; nearly fine. 2

134 1787–88 Cents, 3 of each date, from dies slightly varying from those in the 2 preceding lots. Fair to v. good. 6

4/ **135** 1788 Cents from varying dies, and unlike any of preceding. V. good to nearly fine. 6

(**136 Connecticut.** 1785 Cents, numbered according to Mr. Crosby's arrangement in his work on Early Coins of America. 3 B, C, 4 F, 5 H, 6 F, G, busts *r.* ; 8 D, bust *l.* All mailed busts. In square paste-board coin-holders having circular receptacle, with wine-colored felt paper bottom. Mostly v. good. 7

10 **137** 1786 Cents ; Crosby, 1 A, bust *r.* ; 4 G, 5 B, C, and H, busts *l.* All mailed. Fair to good. 5

138 1787 Cents ; Crosby, 1 A, C, busts *r.* ; 2 B, 4 L, 6 M, 9 E, 11 K, 13 D, 14 H, 15 F*, 16 M, 17 G, 18 G, 19 G, 23 A, 24 G, 30 H, 31 R, busts *l.* Fair to v. good, some approaching fine. 19

// **139** 1787 Others ; C. 31 R, 32 A, X, 33 Q. R, S, T, Z, 37 D ? E, I, K, L, 38 G, L, 41 I, 43 X, Y. Condition about as last. 18

2 4/ **140** 1788 Cents ; C. 1 E, 2 D, 4 K, 8 K, 9 E, 11 G, 12 C, E, F, 13 A*, 14 A*, 15 L, 16 D, N. Fair to about fine. 14

16,00 **141** 1787 AUCTORI CONNEC Mailed bust *r.* ℞ ET LIB INDE Female setd on globe, *right*, holds staff surmounted with Liberty cap in *r.* hand, branch in *l.* Inferior work. Good. 1

I found this piece in a lot from a public sale about 1884, shortly after, it became the property of Col. Cutting. Mr. Wyllys Betts gave it the first notice, and illustrated it in a pamphlet published in 1886. No other specimen, to my knowledge, is known.

5/. **142** Unassorted, 1785, '86, '88.   Poor to v. good ; 1 holed.   21

143 Others, unassorted, 1787.   Poor to very good ; most of last ;
some approaching fine.   22

144 Others quite as last lot.   22

145 **New York.** 1787 EXCELSIOR.   State arms.   ℞ E . PLURIBUS
UNUM ✱   Spread eagle.   Very fair, nearly good.   Very rare.   1

146 1787 Nova Eborac.   Liberty setd *l.*, v. good ; setd *r.*, v. fair.   2

147 1787 Mott's card, thick and thin planchet.   1794 Talbot, Al-
lum & Lee, 3 die var.   Good and v. good.   5

148 THE ' THEATRE ' AT ' NEW ' YORK ' — AMERICA   Front view of
Park Theatre, by *Jacobs.*   ℞ MAY COMMERCE FLOURISH
Two ships *l.* ; emblems of Commerce and cornucopia on
shore ; edge, " I promise to pay on demand the bearer One
Penny."   Unc., partly bright.   Very rare.   1

149 Albany.   CHURCH | 𝕻𝖊𝖓𝖓𝖕 in depression, 17 mlm., on other-
wise blank planchet.   Halfp. size ; holed near edge.   Good,
rare.   1

150 Brooklyn.   Communion Tokens.   Church of the Covenanters,
1857, and Third Reformed Presb'n Cong'n, New York.   V.
fine ; oval.   Lead.   2

151 Castorland.   1796 Franco-Americana Colonia.   Female hd *l.*
Nearly perfect.   1

152 **New Jersey.** (1681) Mark Newbie Farthing and Halfp.
St. Patrick stdg.   ℞ Royal harpist.   V. fair ; scarce.   2

153 1786 Cents.   Bust of a horse *r.* over plow.   ℞ Shield.   Maris,
12 G, 26 S, R ¹, 25 S ; 1787, 29 L ; 1788, 78 dd, R ² In
coin holders.   First poor, remainder good.   5

154 Others, of rarity 3, 1787, CC, 45 d ; of rarity 4, 1786, 16 J,
43 Y, 55 l, 68 w, 74 bb.   Fair to good.   7

155 Others, of rarity 5, 1786, 18 J, v. good ; 24 q, good.   2

156 Others, common and rare, 1786, 14 J, 15 J, 15 L, 15 T, 16 L,
17 b, 17 K, 18 M, 21 N, 21 P, 23 P, 23 R, 24 P ; 1787, 6 D,
28 L, 32 T, 34 J, 37 J.   Fair to very good ; 1 holed.   18

157 Others, graded as last, 1787, 38 c, 38 Y, 38 z, 39 a, 43 d, 44 d,
46 e, 48 g, 52 i, 53 j, 54 k, 56 n, 60 p, 62 q, 63 q, 63 s, 64 t
(2 sizes), 65 u, 67 v.   Fair to very good.   20

The following series, known as "Birmingham Bad Halfpence" by our English
friends, and "Bungtowns" to us, were made in imitation of the Halfpence of Geo. II
and III.   The American Colonies, and later these United States, proved a profitable

market for minters of these impostors of small change. Mr. Crosby cites the act of the Legislature of Pennsylvania, legalizing the circulation of these pieces. They are in coin holders and numbered by my list, which appeared in the Scott Stamp and Coin Company's 16th edition of Copper Catalogue, 1890. The collection is unquestionably the largest ever drawn together in this country. The condition averages good, and it is doubtful if more than a few of them could be improved.

158 **Pennsylvania.** Halfpennies. Auctori Plebis. Bust *r.* and *l.* (the latter 1787). George Reign'd. Glorivs Pellew Charles Fox M. P. Give us Peace. Hispanniola etc.   12

159 Others, varying. Low, 8 to 44.   30

160 Others. L. 50 to 98.   30

161 Others. L. 99 to 157.   30

162 Others. L. 159 to 204.   30

163 Others. L. 205 to 273.   31

164 Others. L. 274 to 302.   30

165 Others. L. 303 to 336.   30

166 Others. L. 337 to 374.   40

167 Farthings, not numbered but all different, and much rarer than the Halfpence.   22

168 **Virginia.** 1773 Halfpenny. Kentucky, n.d., plain edge. V. good.   2

169 Duplicates of Colonials, unassorted. Woods', Vermont, 6 ; Mass., Conn., 2 ; Talbot, A. & L., M. Newbie, New Jersey and Penn., 17 ; Va. and Nova Constellatio. Poor to very good ; 2 holed.   33

170 A similar lot, and fully as desirable, though lacking Mass. and Talbot, A. & L. Poor to v. good.   35

HARD TIMES TOKENS.

171 ANDREW JACKSON Head *r.* ℞ THE BANK MUST PERISH. Wreath. THE | UNION | MUST AND | SHALL. | etc. Low, 1. Fine, very rare.   1

172 FOR THE CONSTITUTION HURRA ! Ship sailing *l.* ℞ Flourish Commerce, etc. WHIGS | OF N. YORK | VICTORIOUS | etc. 1834 Low, 2. In *silver.* Edge obliquely milled. Holed, otherwise fine ; of the highest rarity.   1

    I do not know of another specimen in this metal.

173 Another from same dies as last, in brass, with edge plain. L. 2. Uncirculated ; very rare.   1

174 THE GLORIOUS WHIG VICTORY OF 1834. Liberty cap on rays.
℟ FELLOW CITIZENS SAVE YOUR CONSTITUTION. Ship sail-
ing *r.* L. 3. Very fine ; very rare.   1

175 Another with letters recut, rays heavier and differently arranged. L. 3. In white metal. V. good, nearly fine ; rarer
than the preceding.   1

176 Perish Credit etc. 1834 Boar running *l.* ℟ Bust of Jackson
with narrow shoulders. L. 4. Unc. ; mostly red.   1

177 Another of similar design ; nose of boar points at space bet.
PERISH and CREDIT ℟ Jackson with very broad shoulders.
L. 6. Fine, scarce.   1

178 "A plain system." Jackson walking *l.* L. 8. Fine. Jackson
in safe. ℟ Donkey *l.* L. 16. Unc. Another similar;
donkey has larger body. L. 18. Fine.   3

179 Boar *l.*, same as 176. ℟ Jackson with broad shoulders, same
as 177. L. 7. Slight marks of circulation. Brass, with a
thin coating of silver, as originally issued.   Extremely
rare.   1

180 Jackson in safe. ℟ Donkey stdg *l.*, same as in lot 178, but
in brass. L. 17. V. fine, rare.   1

181 Merchants' Exchange. L. 19, 21, 22. Turtle carrying safe.
℟ Jackass running *l.* L. 24, 25, 26. Good to unc. 3
mostly bright.   6

182 Turtle carrying safe. ℟ Jackass running *l.* The "short
ground" variety. L. 23. Nearly fine ; one of the best specimens I have seen of this rare variety.   1

183 Female head *l.*, laureated ; 13 stars. ℟ MILLIONS FOR DE-
FENCE Wreath. NOT | ONE | CENT | FOR TRIBUTE. L. 27.
Very fine ; by far the choicest I have ever had to offer.
Rare.   1

184 The small head with date bet. 2 small stars. L. 28. "United" head. L. 29. Very good. Another of similar type,
E PLURIBUS UNUM on obv. and *very* small date. L. 30.
None rarer in the series, but this example is considerably
corroded ; date barely visible. A remarkable trio.   3

185 General type of last pc. 6 stars facing. L. 34. V. good. Another with masculine features. L. 35. Good, rare.   2

186 Female head *l.* ℟ Type of 183, *without* dash below *Cent.*
L. 36. Fine, rare.   1

187 Others similar. L. 37, 39, 40 (2 slightly differing, one being the new var. noted in my 2nd ed. ; stem added to leaf opposite first E in DEFENCE ; die otherwise retouched). Good to abt. unc. 2 partly bright. 4

188 Others, Mint Drop (2 var.), etc. All from same obv. die. Female head *l.* L. 41, 42, 43, 44, 45. Good to fine. 5

189 ✱ VAN BUREN ✱ — METALLIC 1837 CURRENCY Wrecked ship. ℞ MILLIONS FOR DEFENCE etc. Wreath, 3 berries outside, 6 inside, no dash below CENT. L. 46. Fine but very dark ; exceedingly rare ; in but few cabinets ; has an auction record of $25.00. 1

190 Jackson in safe. ℞ Wrecked ship. L. 49. Phoenix rising from flames, with four dif. revs. L. 50, 51, 52, 53. Also, Half | Cent | worth | of | Pure Copper. L. 54. Good to v. fine. 6

191 A FRIEND — TO THE CONSTITUTION A steer *r.* ℞ AGRICULTURE AND COMMERCE A ship *r.* L. 56. Fine, scarce. 1

192 J GIBBS MANUFACTURER — BELLEVILLE in field, OF | MEDALS | AND | TOKENS | &C | N. J ℞ Ship, as last. L. 57. V. good, rare. 1

193 W. GIBBS AGRICULTUREIST — N. YORK A bouquet of flowers. ℞ Same as obv. of 191. L. 58. Good, v. rare. A fine one in the Betts sale brought $8.50. 1

194 T. D. SEAMAN BUTCHER — BELLEVILLE. A bouquet sim. to last. ℞ Same as. 191. L. 59. Good, rare. 1

195 Dayton's card. L. 61. Good. Centre Market. L. 66, 67. Jarvis' card. L. 68, 69. All with head *l.* Fine to unc. 4 are partly bright. 5

196 The masculine head *l.* ℞ Crossman and Maycock card ; the latter also with eagle. L. 62, 64, 65. Uncirculated ; partly bright. 3

197 Abraham Riker's card, with ℞ NOT | ONE | CENT etc. 2 differing. L. 70, 71 (NOT erased). V. good, scarce. 2

198 Ezra B. Sweet. ℞ Type of 1837 Cent. L. 72 (the thick planchet). V. fine. 1

199 Devau's card. Feuchtwanger's Cent (4 var.) Woman and sister. Loco Foco head. L. 74, 78, 79, 80. Good. 5

200 Arms of the State of New York, 1837. ℞ Feuchtwanger's. Three Cents. Wreath. L. 75. V. fine. 1

201 "The sober second thoughts," etc. Bust of Van Buren *l.* L.
     81, 82. Holed, as all are ; otherwise fine. Copper and
     brass. Rare.   2

202 * WEBSTER * — CREDIT 1841 CURRENT Ship sailing *r.* 4 va-
     rieties, with 5 different revs. L. 84, 85, 86, 88, 89, 90. Very
     choice (excepting 86) ; partly bright to full red.   6

203 Obv. same as L. 84. ℞ * VAN BUREN * METALLIC 1837 CUR-
     RENCY Wrecked ship, lightning above. L. 87. Uncircu-
     lated, much original redness ; excels all specimens of this
     number I have seen. I pronounce it matchless ; it is
     extremely rare in any condition. A gem of the first
     water.   1

204 Head *l.* ℞ Ship. L. 91 (rare). A dif. head *l.*, branches in
     place of stars, with 3 dif. revs. L. 91, 92, 93, 94. Good to
     v. fine.   4

205 1864 Eagle, wings spread, holds serpent in his talons. ℞
     Feuchtwanger's 3 | THREE | CENTS From same die as L. 77.
     Extremely fine, rare.   1

206 Duplicates of the preceding. L. 16, 17 (brass), 25, 37, 52, 66,
     84, 85. Very fair to very fine ; most of last.   9

207 Turtle and Jackass, short ground var. L. 23. Fair, very rare.
     Ship. ℞ Wreck, "Metallic Currency." L. 87. Poor but
     extremely rare.   2

208 Ship. ℞ Wreck, "Currency," same as 203. L. 87. Nearly
     fine ; extremely rare.   1

209 Baltimore Tokens. Fasces bet. cornucopias. ℞ Anchor,
     without date or inscription. Brass, 17½ (very rare) ; Æ, 21.
     Fine.   2

210 Howell Works Garden (N. J.) Size, Haskins' "Not One Cent
     but just as good." etc., size of old Cent, and 9 War Tokens,
     Brooklyn Bridge medals, etc. Good to fine ; 3 holed, as
     issued.   19

HALF CENTS.

212 1793, '94, '95, '97. Poor, excepting '95, which is about good.   4
213 1800, '03, '04, '05. Uncommonly good to fine.   4
214 1802 Dent on rev. slightly raises top of head on obv., other-
     wise nearly fine ; a most uncommon condition. Rare.   1
215 1806, '07, '08, '09, '10 (scarce), '11 (rare). Very good.   6

216 1825, '26, '28, '29, '32, '33, '34, '35. Very fine to about unc.
Desirable. 8
217 1849, '50, '51, '53, '54, '55, '56, '57. Fine. 8

CENTS.

218 1793 Chain, " America." Good, rare. 1
219 1793 Chain ; period after date and Liberty. Fair ; date good. 1
220 1793 Wreath ; vine and bars on edge. Good. 1
221 1794, '95 (value in centre of wreath, also high), '96, Lib. cap
and fillet head. V. fair to good ; the better prevail. 5
222 1797, '98 (2 var.), 1800, '01. Good and very good. 5
223 1799 Good, a medium brown color. The rarest date in the
series. 1
224 1802 Very fine ; medium olive. 1
225 1802 (3 var., 1 without stems), '03, '05, '06, '07 (2 var.), '08.
Fair to v. good. 9
226 1803 Very fine, well centered ; medium olive. 1
227 1804 A beautiful and strong impression ; obv. a *trifle* off from
centre ; medium dark olive. 1
This cent appears to have once had a slight corrosion. It has been artistically treat-
ed, and requires a searching gaze to detect this, so well does it assimilate original
sharpness. From the Foster Ely sale at $25.00; a previous record of the piece is re-
ported at $50.00.
228 1809 Very good ; the date is particularly strong. Rare. 1
229 1810, '11 (very fair), '12, '14. Good. 4
230 1813 Fine. A faint scratch before chin. 1
231 1816 Uncirculated, partly bright. 1
232 1817, '18 (2 var.), '19, '20 (2 var.), '21. Good to unc. 7
233 1822, '23, '24, '24, '25, '27, '29, '30, '31, '33, '35 (2 var.), '36.
Fair to good. 12
234 1826 A sharp, even impression ; scarcely less than uncirculated ; slight scratch on rev. Medium olive. 1
235 1828, '34, '38. Fine. 3
236 1832 Only slight indications of circulation ; a little discolora-
tion on obv. A light olive. 1
237 1837 Plain and beaded hair-cord ; very choice light olives.
Barely impaired by circulation. 2
238 1839 Booby head (or short-haired). Uncirculated, bright red.
Found in a Pittsfield bank, where it had probably laid since
year of coinage. 1

239 1839 Head of '38. Silly head (hair on forehead extends be-
     yond profile line). Both fine.   2

240 1839 Head of '40, '40 (2 var.), '41, '42 (2 var.), '43 (2 var.),
     '45, '46, '48, '49, '51, '53, '55 (2 var.) Fair to fine.   16

241 1844 Very fine, slight scratches ; light olive.   1

242 1847, '50, '52, '54 (spotted), '56 (2 var.) V. fine to unc. ; some
     are bright.   6

243 1854 Pattern Cent. Lib. hd *l.*, no stars. Unc., partly bright.   1

244 1855 Pattern Cent. Flying eagle. Unc., red.   1

245 1857 Small and large date. V. good.   2

246 **Small Cents.** 1856 Nickel. Flying eagle. Very fine, bril-
     liant, probably never in circulation. Very rare ; a much-
     coveted Cent, and steadily advancing in price.   1

247 1857 to 1883, consecutive. Unc. and proof ; most of last.   28

248 **Two Cents.** 1864 Small and large letters in motto (2) to
     1873. Two are fine, others unc. to proof (3 of last).   11

249 **Nickel Three Cents.** 1866 to 1883, consecutive. 8 are
     fine to unc., remainder proof.   19

250 **Nickel Five Cents.** 1866 to '83, lacking 1878. Fine to
     proof ; many of the best.   20

251 Duplicates. 1873 Proof, and 12 Cents, including a very fair
     1809. Half Cent, 1828.   14

WEST INDIA ISLANDS.

252 **Bermudas.** SOMMER ISLANDS. A hog *l.*, above VI ℞ A
     ship *l.* Good ; extremely rare. 26.   1

253 Shilling, same type. XII above hog. Good ; extremely rare.
     32.   1

254 Geo. III. 1793 Halfpenny. Bust. ℞ Ship. Bzd proof.   1

255 **Bahama.** Geo. III. 1806 Halfp. Bust. ℞ Ship. Gilt proof,
     slight blemishes.   1

256 **Barbadoes.** 1788 Penny. Negro head *l.*, I SERVE Pine-
     apple. Struck with a collar, milled borders. Unc., partly
     bright. Very rare.   1

257 1788 Others from varying dies ; also the Penny of 1792. Good
     to fine.   3

258 1792 Penny. Obv. from same die as 256. ℞ King setd
     in marine car *l.* Milled borders. Unc., bril., dark. Very
     rare.   1

259 1792 Halfpenny type as last, also with milled borders. Unc. ;
most parts bright. Very rare.   1

260 Moses Tolanto — Barbadoes. A bale. ℞ Freedom without
slavery. A cask. A deep oblong punch on rev. (a mark
commonly found upon Mr. T.'s tokens), otherwise fine. A
light olive. Extremely rare. Farthing. 22.   1

261 M. Tolanto. Halfpenny, type as last. Good. 29.   1

262 Thomas Lawlor & C? | 11 | Broad S! | Bridgetown | Barba-
does. ℞ General | Merchants | and | Commission Agents.
Fine ; extremely rare. 21½.   1

263 Jamaica. William Smith "in Kingston." Halfpenny and
Penny. Fine and rare, especially the smaller piece.   2

264 M. Howard — Ferry Grass. Coach. ℞ Kingston — Jamaica.
Saddled horse. 29. Thos. Lundie & Co. 1844. Steamship.
Brass. 23. Both good. Victoria. 1871 Halfp. and Penny.
Uncirculated. Nickel.   4

265 Cuba. Eden Park, 2½, 5 Ctvs. Esperanza, 2½, 5, 10 do. V.
R. & Co., Gibara, Havana, O'Reilly, 13. Æ, brass and
nickel. Unc. 19 to 29.   7

266 Havana. C. R. S. & Co., Lobeck, 2½, 5 Ctvs. Maragliano,
2½, 5, 10 do. Matanzas, Labayen y Hermano. 1 fine, others
unc. Æ, brass and nickel. 21 to 40.   7

266a Porto Rico. Hacienda Stᵃ Catalina 1881 ¼, ½ and 1 D.
By Barras y Hermanos. Fine. Tin, 16, 18, 23.   3

267 Haiti. HENRI CHRISTOPHER, President, 1807. Mil. bust
facing. ℞ UNE | CENTIEME etc. Unc., light olive. Very
rare. 26.   1

268 1812 HENRICUS DEI GRATIA HAITI REX. Bust *r.*, below, ESSAY
℞ Deus Causa . etc. Cwnd arms. Very fine and rare. Æ,
28½.   1

269 An 27 = 1830. Head of J. P. Boyer *l.* ℞ Arms, etc. Usual
type. 100 Ctms. struck over U. S. Cent of 1833. Fine.   1

270 Centimes, 1830, '31, '32, '40, '41. Two Ctms., 1829, '30, '31,
'40, '41, '42. Good to fine.   11

271 Varieties of the 1 and 2 Ctms. in last lot. Poor to fine.   18

272 L. Pierrot, 1846, 1, 2, and 6¼ Ctms. Fasces type ; the last
rare. Fine.   3

273 J. B. Riché, 1846, 1, 2, and 6 Ctms. Faustin, 1849, 2 and 6
Ctms. ; 1850, Emperor, 2 and 6¼ do. Good to fine.   7

274 Geffrard, 1863, 5, 10, 20 Centimes. Brilliant, red proofs. V.
rare.   3

275 1 and 2 Ctms., issues of 1881 and '86. Unc., red; 1 a little
stained.   4

276 1877 Patterns, 10 and 20 Ctms. (the first in nickel), and 3
others of Faustin, unofficial. All proofs.   5

277 **Port au Prince.** A. T. | & B. R. ℞ GLACIERE | PORT AU
PRINCE Fine. W.m. 27.   1

278 **San Domingo.** F. 7 Cwnd. ¼ Rl., also S. D. ℞ Anchor,
the latter in lead, size 23, and attribution uncertain. V. good.   2

279 A var. of first in last lot, also ¼ Real, 1844, '48, very good, and
patterns, 1877 1 (2 var.), 2 and 2½ Ctvs. Unc. Æ, brass
and nickel.   7

280 1878 Other patterns, 1 and 2 Ctvs., each with value in large
and small letters. Proofs, 25, 31. 1882 2½ Ctvs., nickel,
of regular coinage.   5

281 **Danish W. I.** Chris. VI. 1740 I and II Skilling. Monogram cwnd. ℞ DE DANSK. AMERIC etc. V. good and fine;
rare. 1764 24 Sk., ship type, and Cents, 1859, '60, '68.
Good to unc.   6

282 **French Colonies.** Louis XVIII. 5 and 10 Ctms., modern essais, brilliant and var. dates of 5 and 10 Ctms. of
Chas. X and L. Phil. Fair to fine.   10

283 L. Philippe. 1843 5 Ctms. 1844 5 and 10 do. Unc., red;
a very rare condition.   3

284 **Antigua.** St. Eustatius, Herman Gossling, 1771; also S E
and P, T. B (Tobago), M and fleur-de-lis (Martinique).
Last 3 CS. on Cayenne Sous. Good; a rare lot.   5

285 **Trinidad.** J. G. D'Ade & Cº ℞ ONE | FARTHING | TOKEN
Fine and very rare.   1

MEXICO.

286 Chas. and his mother Joanna. Quarto of earliest American
coinage. Mint established 1535. Holed; good. 31.   1

287 Chas. III. 1768 1/16 Real. C and S linked and cwnd. Fine;
extremely rare. Brass. 21.   1

287a Ferd. VII. (1813) Supreme Junta, ½ Real. Eagle on arched
oval. ℞ Bow, etc. Very fair, extremely rare. Not in Fis.
or Fon. 16.   1

288 Ferd. VII. $\frac{1}{8}$, $\frac{1}{4}$ and $\frac{2}{4}$; of the last, 1815, '16, '21 ; also dbl.
Quarto, Revolutionary period (without date).   Fair to
good.   6

289 Republic. $\frac{1}{16}$ (2), $\frac{1}{8}$ (4), $\frac{1}{4}$ (8) Reals, 1829–36.   Good to fine ;
several scarce.   14

290 1836 Pattern Quartilla. Liberty cap. ℞ Eagle. Proof ; rare.
27.   1

291 1842 Octavo. Liberty setd. Very fine, partly bright. 1863
Ctvo. Good. Empire, 1864, Ctvo. Fair.   3

292 1863 Ctvo. in lead, plain edge. 1868 Ctvos., brass silvered,
and Æ. Proofs from the Fischer collection. Rare.   3

293 Centavos from Ṃ mint, 1870–78, '80, '81, '86, '87, '89 ; N. C.
mint, 1874, '77, '80, '81. Good to unc.   18

294 **States and Cities.** Chihuahua. $\frac{1}{4}$ Real, 1834, '46, '55, '56.
Indian with bow and arrow. 1860, '65, '66 Liberty setd.
Good to fine.   7

295 Cocula. 1825 $\frac{1}{8}$ Real, " A common benefit by the Municipal-
ity." Eagle on cactus plant. Fair, very rare. 22.   1

296 Cocupao. 1848 $\frac{1}{8}$ Real, MUNICIPAL etc. A cluster of trees.
℞ $\frac{1}{8}$ below clasped hands. Good, very rare. 23.   1

297 Durango. 1822 $\frac{1}{8}$ Real. Prov. of Nueva Vizcaya. 1824 $\frac{1}{8}$ do.
Eagle. ℞ LIBERTAD on band below rays. Good ; both
rare, the latter especially so.   2

298 1828 $\frac{1}{8}$ Real. Lib. cap. ℞ Indian boy before tree. Good,
very rare. 1847 $\frac{1}{8}$ do., large 8. V. fair.   2

299 1858 *Brass.* 1860 " Libertad," etc. 1866 " Independencia,"
etc. 1872 " Sufragio Libre." All $\frac{1}{4}$ Reals. The last fine
and very rare.   4

300 Guadalajara (place of mintage). 1838 Pattern Quartilla. Lib-
erty head. ℞ 1 | QUARTILLA | Gᵃ within cartouch. Unc. ;
very rare. Brass. 30.   1

301 Centavos of the Republic. Gᵃ below date on rev. 1872 to
'78, '81. Good to fine ; difficult to obtain.   8

302 Guanaxuato. 1828 Quartilla. Female setd. ℞ Lib. cap. V.
good. 1829 Octavo, same type. V. good. Both rare and
in brass. 28, 21.   2

303 1856 Cuartilla. Eagle. ℞ Arms in oval. 1857 Octavo and
Cuart., same type. Last 2 in brass. Centavos of the Rep.
Gᵒ below date, 1878, '80. Good to unc.   5

304 Hermosillo. 1834, '35, '36 Cuartillas. Lib. cap. ℞ Arrow
      bet. quivers. Fair and scarce. Ctvs. of the Rep. H° below
      date, 1880, '81. Good.   5

305 Jalisco. Octavos, 1828, '29 ; Quartos, 1829, '31, '33, '34, '35,
      '36. Good, some approaching fine.   8

306 Medio Octavos, 1860, '61 ;   Octavos, 1856-60 ;   Departa-
      mento, 1860, '61, '62. Estado. Cuartillas, 1858-62. Good
      to fine.   15

307 Oaxaca. The coinage of General Morelos. 1812 1, 2
      and 8 Reals. Monogram of Morelos. ℞ SUD below
      bow and arrow. Very good ; the first very rare. 20, 29,
      30.   3

308 1812 Varieties of 2 Reals and 8 Reals, CS. Good.   3

309 1813 2 (2 var., one with figure 2 punched) and 8 Reals, the
      latter CS. V. good ; fine for the coinage.   3

310 1813 8 Reals. Strong impression from a boldly executed die,
      with broad milled borders. Fine. 40.   1

311 1813 8 Reals, similar to preceding, with floral designs intro-
      duced. Fine.   1

312 1813 8 Rls. ℞ Straight top bow, below * T * C * | * SUD *
      Fine and rare.   1

313 San Luis Potosi. 1828 ¼ Real. A strong impression ; I have
      never seen its equal.   1

314 Others. ¼ Rls., 1829, '30, '32, '59. V. good, and a poor ⅛ Rl.
      of 1859 ; also, Ctvs. of the Rep. 1863, S. L. P. ; '77, '78, P.
      Good.   8

315 Sinaloa. ¼ Reals, 1855, '59, '61–66. Sonora. Large Cuar-
      tillas, 1859, '61, '62, '63. V. good.   12

316 Tapalpa. 1856 A Liberty cap. ℞ COMERCIO DE TAPALPA ·
      In field, ⅛. Tecolatlan. ⅛ Real by the Municipality 184(?).
      Tlazasalca. ⅛ Real (1853). Fair to good ; all very rare. 21
      to 24.   3

317 Yucatan, Campeche. 1861 Ctvo. Good, scarce.   1

318 Merida. 1856 ⅛ Grano de Peso. V. fair. 26. 1860 Cento
      de Real. Good. Oval, 14 x 18. Lead.   2

319 Motul. CIUDAD DE MOTUL 1879 ⅛ Real. Good, rare. Lead.
      22.   1

320 Temax. VILLA | DE | TEMAX ⅛ Real, 18(71). Good, rare.
      Lead. 23.   1

321 Zacatecas. Octavos, 1851, '58, '59, '62, '63 ; Quartillas, 1825, '36, '46, '52, '58, '59, '62, '63. Fair to very choice. Ctvs. of the Republic. Z? below date, 1873–78, '80, '81. V. good. Zamora. ⅛ Real, CS.   21

322 1838 Pattern Cuartilla. Liberty head. ℞ UNA | CUARTILLA | z? within wreath. Unc. ; a few light spots. Rare. 30.   1

323 Varieties of the preceding, among which, Chihuahua, Durango, 1828 ; Guanaxuato, 1828, '57 ; Morelos (1 and 2 Reals), etc. Mostly good, quite equal to those they follow ; 1 holed.   39

Hacienda Pieces and Tokens issued by Merchants.

324 Ahualulco, Plaza del Mercado. Var. of ⅛ Real, one dated 1826 ; Amajac, P. L., 1886 ; Ameca, various ⅛ and ¼ Reals, 1826–55, etc. ; Apatcingan, M. E., 1850. Mostly good.   9

325 Buena Vista, 1855, J. F. V. Colima ; 1855, Y. B. Del Plan (3) ; Medina, 1820 ; Jalisco, 1824 ; La Barca, 1857, etc. Mostly good, 2 in lead, some large.   12

326 Mexico. Lohse (2 var.), Felix, Monterey, "Don't forget Alex." ; Puga, 1871 ; Quitupan, 1854, etc. Mostly fine.   8

327 Sonora. M. Yingo, ¼ Real, brass ; fine. 19. 1 Real, Æ and Æ, unc. 24. Eagle, type sim. to coinage of the Rep. Rare.   3

328 Tuxpango. 5 and 10 Ctvs., Fis., 367, 368. Uncommon. Brass ; 25, 30. Vera Cruz, by Velasco. Zahuay, 1856 ; a wolf l. Hermanos, tin. 25. Another, ANO | DE | 1836 ℞ PENY | CHET CS. q. Good to fine. 27.   5

329 Others, localities unknown. Heart, Dog ? and lozenge shape, none circular, all probably of last century. A very interesting, curious and rare lot. Mostly fine.   12

330 Others quite as indefinite, all in monograms ; one dated 1773 in Roman numerals. From Fis. collection, 690, 691, 693, 697, 701. None circular. Good. 21 to 34.   5

331 Others with monogram, round planchets. From Fis. coll'n, 686, 687, 692, 694, 695, 698, 699, 700. Also 3 in lead, probably by merchants in Yucatan, of a later period. Good. 20 to 27.   11

332 Others, monograms, initials and names. From Fis. coll'n, 702 to 712, etc. Fair to good. 19 to 28.   12

333 Others with names. 2 bear dates 1790 and 1793. All round, mostly good. 16 to 27.   12

334   Costa Rica. ¼ Centavo, without date. Fine, extremely rare. 13.   1
335   Toledo. Hacienda St. Rosa, 1864, San Isidro. A steamship
      r. San Ysidro, by J. A. C. 1877, San Jose and San Juan,
      Guatemala, 1871, Ctvo. Fine. Æ and brass.   6
336   Honduras. 1, 2, 4 and 8 Reals, 1851–57, Necessity pcs, and
      the best specimens forming a set that I have seen. 20, 39.   4
337   Others of same issue, 4 Reals, 1851, '53, '54, '56, '57 (2), '59 ;
      8 do., 1856, '58, '59. Poor to fine.   10
338   1862 1, 2, 4 and 8 Pesos, Necessity pcs, in copper, from dies
      for gold coins. Good to fine, rare. 19 to 40.   4
339   1870 ⅛ and ¼ Real, nickel ; 1879 Lib. head, Ctvo. and 10 and
      25 Ctvs. Zelaya i Diaz, Balize, ¼ Real, 1871, by J. J. The
      last 3 in brass. British Hond. 1885 Cent. Fine. 15 to 28.   7
340   Nicaragua. 1860 REPUBLICA DE NICARAGUA In field, UN |
      CENTABO | 1860 ℞ LIBERTAD Y UNION. Three mountain
      peaks. Unc. ; extremely rare. 25.   1
340a — Leon. A lion rampant l. ℞ N R (joined) ¼, a star above
      and below. Milled borders. Fine. Very rare. 13.   1

This piece, without date, I believe to have been struck in time of Ferd. VII, and
between the years 1810 and 1815.

341   1878 Centavo, in nickel. 1883 Cojutepeque Leon. Tokens
      by the Market for ₃⁄₄ and ₁⁄₂ Dime. Wounta, 10 Ctvs., by
      G. S. and S., etc. Fine to unc.   6

SOUTH AMERICA.

342   **U. S. Colombia.** Colombia Farthings. Bust r. (15), bust
      l. (2). Believed to be all different. Fine.   17
343   Carthagena. 1812 and '13, ½ Real, and 2 Reals, date invisi-
      ble. Indian setd beside cabin. Also, 2 Reals of Pillar
      type, struck over same coin. Fair to v. good.   4
344   Varieties of the 3 coins in the preceding lot. Fair to good.   9
345   Colon. S. Soracco, Am de la quadra, Velez. Santa Marta.
      Ferd. VII, 1813, large S. M. (2 var.) ; 1820, ¼ Real (2 var.)
      Mostly good.   7
346   ESQUINA | DEL | VERDE A cannon l. ℞ VALE MITAD | MAN-
      UEL ANGULO Fine workmanship. Unc. ; very desirable. 29.   1
347   New Granada. 1847 ½ and 1 Dcmo. ; 1848 ½ do. Ecuador.
      1872 1 and 2 Ctvos. Good to fine.   5

348 **Peru.** 1822 ¼ Real, "Provisional." Sun in rays. 16. 1823
⅛ and ¼ Peso. Sun, mts. and llama. 20, 27. Good, scarce.   3
349 1855 Medio Centavo of Lima. Fine and rare. 1864-78 Ctvs.
(4), Dos Ctvs. (5). Good to fine.   10
350 Arequipa. 20 Ctvs. by M. Forga. A crater. Callao, Hotel
Ytaliano, 1863. Cancte, 1 and 2 Ctvs. by Enrique Swayne
and others, without name of place; believed to be Callao
and Lima. Good to v. fine.   13
351 Coto, 25 Ctvs. Diez, 10 Ctvs. Urizar y Ca., 1876, Esperanza (saltpetre mines), 10 Ctvs. La Pena, 20 do. Lima,
various (one with Cristobal Colon). Good to fine.   12
352 Lota, 10 Ctvs. A steamship. Santa, 1878, 10, 20 Ctvs.
(nickel). Santander, 1874, Ste. Maria y Lappe (saltpetre
mines), 1 Peso. Tacna Union Club; also set of Prov. Soc'y
(3). Æ, brass and nickel. Good to unc. 18 to 29.   9
353 **Bolivia.** LA UNION | ES LA | FUERZA | POTOSI 1864 ℞ 1 |
CENTECI | MO Fine, v. rare. 20½.   1
354 1868 20 Ctvs., from dies for silver coins. 1883 1 and 2 Ctvs.
Essais. Unc.   3
355 1878 Republic Bolivia. Condor. 1 and 2 Ctvs. Fine, rare.
20, 23.   2
356 Cochabamba, LaPaz, Oruro,·etc. Issues by merchants; fine
work; 4 are unc. Brass and nickel. 15 to 25.   5
357 **Chile.** 1835 "Dump" Centavo. Unc., red; a gem. 22.   1
358 1835 Ctvo.; 1851 and '53, ½ and 1 do.; 1879 to '87, various
dates of ½, 1, 2 and 2½ Ctvs. Good to fine.   15
359 1836 8 Escudo, from dies for gold coins, milled edge. Fine.
35. 1851 Essai medalets; also Catatilco token for 20 Ctvs. 4
360 **Venezuela.** 1812 ¼ Real, 1·9. within 12 mlm circle on ra-
diation, terminating in 7 points. Holed, otherwise good;
rare. 28.   1
361 Another of same design, 1·9. on 15 mlm circle. Good; rare.
30.   1
362 1843 ¼, ½, 1 Ctvo. 1852 Same values, with var. of the Ctvo.
1858 and '62 Ctvs. Good to unc. 1863 Essai 1 and 2 Ctvs.
with head l. Unc.   11
363 Caracas. ⅛ Real, 1818, very rare; ¼ do., 1813, '14, '16, '17,
'18, '21; also tokens of Carabobo, Montalban and Zambrano.
Good to fine; some of last unc.   13

364 1813–21 Varieties of ¼ Real in preceding lot. Good to fine.   20
365 **British Guiana.** Geo. III. 1813 1 Stiver. Unc. ; light
     olive. I never saw another approaching its equal, or a more
     beautiful impression of any copper coin.   1
366 1813 Half Stvr. ; 1838 1 do. Spanish Guiana. Ferd. VII,
     ½ Reals, 1813, '14, '15, '16. French Guiana. 1782 to 1887,
     the last an unofficial essai. Good to fine.   11
367 **Dutch Guiana.** (Suriname) 1679 1, 2 and 4 Doits. Parrot
     on branch. A very rare set. 1764 Doit. Coffee plant.
     Fine. 16 to 22.   4
368 Varieties of the two preceding lots, including 2 and 4 Doits of
     1679. Good to fine.   12
369 **Brazil.** JOHANNES V (problematical, there are other ver-
     sions). Portuguese arms. ℞ A globe. Fair. Lead.
     27.   1
370 John V, Jos. I, Maria and Peter, John, P. R., and John VI.
     Various years and denominations from V to LXXX Reis.
     None counterstamped ; Rio mint, and without mint marks.
     Not easily gathered. Mostly very good.   37
371 John, P. R. 1809 Pattern 960 Reis. From same dies as
     Meili, plate 37, No. 7 (in Æ). A bronzed proof. V. rare.
     41.   1
372 Counterstamped with arms of Portugal on obv. John V, 1718,
     to Maria I, 1796. Various years and denominations from
     V to XL Reis ; one of the last also CS. on rev. Mostly
     good to fine.   28
373 Peter I, 1823, to Republic, 1889. 20 to 80 Reis and 10 to 200
     Reis. Many fine to unc. None counterstamped.   33
374 The counterstamped of Peter I, reduced to 10, 20 and 40 Reis.
     Good.   10
375 *Bahia.* 1765 V Reis ; 1809, '12, XL do. ; 1813 XX do. ;
     1816 XX, XL do. ; 1820 LXXX do. ; 1821 XX, LXXX do. ;
     1822 X do. ; 1825 80 do. Good to fine ; none CS. ; some
     are rare.   11
376 *Ceara.* C-E-A-R-A within 5-pointed star ; CS. on Rio 20 Reis,
     1825. V. fine and rare ; a gem.   1
377 A similar CS. on Rio 80 Reis, 1827. Good, rare.   1
378 Another as last, CS. over a previous one for Maranhao. Good,
     rare.   1

379 *Cuyaba.* Mint mark C, sizes smaller than die or Bahia. 1824
40 Reis ; 1825 40 do., CS. to 10 ; 1826 80 do., CS. to 20 ;
1828 40 do., another CS. to 10, 80 do. ; 1828 40 do., CS.
to 10, also 80 do. ; also a large C, CS. on Caracas 1821 ¼ R.
Good to fine, none common.   9

380 *Goyas.* Mint mark G, sizes sim. to Ceara. 1827 Very fine.
1829 Very fair. 1830 (CS. to 10 R.), all 40 Reis.
Scarce.

381 *Maranhao.* A large M, CS. on arms side of 80 R., Rio mint,
1832. Fine, rare.   1

382 M | xx CS. on value side of 1827 Rio 80 R. Fine, rare.   1

383 As last, though from dif. die on 1830 Rio 80 R. Fine. Sao
Paulo. 1828 80 R. V. fine ; light olive. Rare.   2

384 *Minas Geraes.* Mint mark M. John VI, 1819 37½ Reis.
Fine, very rare.   1

385 1819 75 Reis, figure of value erased ; 1821 37½ do. Fine.
Peter I, 1828 37½ do. V. fair. All rare.   3

386 1825 Peter I, 37½ Reis. V. good ; v. rare.   1

387 **Argentine** Conf. 1854 1, 2, 4 Ctvs. Good. Rep., 1883 1
Ctvo. ; '84, 2 do. ; '85, 1, 2 do. Fine. Also 3 unofficial
essais.   10

388 Buenos Ayres. 1822–31 various 5, 10 and 20 Decimos. Good
to v. fine. 23 to 32.   7

389 1840 5/10, 1, 2 Rls. ; 1844 2 do. ; 1853, '54, '55, '56 (date in
wrth), 2 Rls. ; 1860, '61, date and value in wrth. Good to
fine.   10

390 Coliseo de Buenos Ayres. Harp, etc. ℞ ENTRADA | COMEDIA
CS. with a P and fleur-de-lis. Good. 33. Also, tramway
card in nickel. Fine.   2

391 **Uruguay.** 1840, '43, 20 Ctmos. ; 1844, 5, 20, 40 do. Bril-
lado, a merchant's token for 50 Ctvs. Brass. 28. Good
to v. fine ; partly bright. A scarce lot.   6

392 1854 20 Ctmos. Poor. 1857 5, 20, 40 do. Fine. 1869 1, 2,
4 do. Unc. ; bright red.   8

393 **Paraguay.** 1845 1/12 Real ; 1870 1, 2, 4 Ctmos. The last
piece is *without* ribbons tying stems of branches, which form
wreath, and is very rare. Good to fine.   4

394 1870 4 Centesimos, usual type, *with* ribbons fastening stems.
Uncirculated ; bright red. 35.   1

395 An unofficial Essai for 2 Ctvs., 1868, and an impostor, purporting to be 2 Ctvs. of Patagonia, 1874. Both bright red. 2
396 Merchants' tokens and Hacienda pcs., location undetermined. Arjona, Carmen, Carrizal, by Dublin Matos ; Colonia, San Carlo, etc. One with bust. Good to unc. 18 to 32. 12
397 Others, sets or partial. Asturias, Belin, Carimao, Guayanilla, Lira, etc. Unc. 19 to 32. 18
398 Others with names or initials only. Good to unc. ; 1 holed. 10 to 39. 21
399 Duplicates of West Indies, Mexico, Central and So. America, including Barbadoes, Havana, Durango, Honduras (1862), Paraguay. Mostly v. good. 56
400 Another selection, equally as good, contains Bermuda, Antigua, Nueva Viscaya, Jalisco, Uruguay, etc. Mostly good. 51

GREAT BRITAIN.

401 **England.** Early British. Head. ℞ Horse. Good. Stycæ of Eanred and Aethelred. Both fine. Chas. I, Farthing. Good. 4
402 Chas. II, 1665, Farthing. Gilt. 23. Also, Halfpenny without date. 33. Both patterns, very fine and rare. 2
403 Ship *l.* ℞ SOLI DEO GLORIA St. George on dragon. Very good ; a rare pattern Hlfp. without date. 29. 1
404 1673 Farthing. V. fine. 22. Hlfp. Nearly fine, but date weak. 29. 2
405 Other Farthings, 1672, '74, '75, with 5 varieties of Chas. I Farthings. Good to fine. 8
406 Jas. II, 1685 (on edge). Tin Farthing, copper plug in centre. V. good, rare. 22. 1
407 1686 Another from a dif. die, good ; also a Pattern Farthing of Mary II. ℞ A rose. V. good. 2
408 Wm. and Mary. Bust of Wm. III *r.* ℞ Bust of Mary II *r.* Pattern Hlfp. without date. V. fine and rare. 29. 1
409 1690 (on edge). Tin Hlfp., copper plug. Fine, rare. 29. 1
410 1694 Farthing and Hlfp. Very fine. 2
411 Wm. III. Bust *r.* ℞ NON DEVIO Sun and rays. Pattern Farthing, planchet composed of half copper and half brass, vertical division. Good ; extremely rare. 22. 1

412 1696 Farthing and Hlfp. Nearly fine. 2
413 1697 Halfpenny. Britannia setd., date below. Unc., partly
bright ; rev. a little weak. 1
414 1699 Another with date in legend. Unc., partly bright. 1
415 1699 Farthing and Hlfp. (head on rev. weak), dates in exergue.
Fine. 2
416 Farthings, 1697 (2 var.), '99, date in legend (poor) ; Hlfp.,
1698, 1700, 'or, with a variety of Wm. and Mary Farthing,
1694. Fair to v. good. 7
417 Anne. 1714 Farthing. Bust *l.* ℞ Britannia setd *l.* Fine
and rare. 21. 1
418 Pattern Halfpenny without date. Bust *l.*, with titles. ℞ The
queen setd *l.* beneath a crown, without legend. Very good,
very rare. 28. Also the reverse of another (obv. ground
off), rose and thistle on stems entwined beneath crown. Fair. 2
419 Geo. I. 1719 Hlfp. 1720 Farthing. Unc., partly bright. 2
420 Farthings, 1717, '19, '21, '22, '24. Hlfp., 1717, '18, '20 to '24.
Good to fine. 12
421 Geo. II. Young head, Far., 1735 ; Hlfp., 1730 ; old head,
Far., 1749 ; Hlfp., 1748. Geo. III. Far., 1773 ; Hlfp., 1771.
All v. fine and choice. 6
422 Differing dates of Farthings (13) and Halfpence (27) of Geo.
II and III, including the rare GEORIVS . III Halfpenny.
Many fine. 40
423 Geo. III. 1788 Pattern Hlfp. by *Droz.* Bust *r.* ℞ BRITAN-
NIA . 1788. Edge, guilloche pattern. A bronzed proof,
slightly impaired. Rare. 1
424 1788 Another. Bust shorter, D. F. on truncation. ℞ From
same die as last. Edge, " Render to Casar the things which
are Cesars " (sic). A gilt proof, slightly impaired. Rare. 1
425 1790 Another. Bust *r.* *Droz F* on truncation. ℞ Britannia
holds spear in *l.* hand. Edge, guilloche pattern. Bronzed
proof. Rare. 1
426 1790 Another. *Droz F* below bust. ℞ From same die as
last. Edge plain. Fine ; some nicks. Rare. 1
427 1797 Pattern Far., Halfp., Penny and Twopence, by *Küchler.*
The Halfp. has oblique milling in centre of edge ; the remainder have plain edges. Gilt proofs, with some trifling
blemishes. 4

/ /ᶜ **428** 1797 Penny and Twopence from same dies as last two in preceding lots (the accepted designs). V. fine ; the first partly bright.   2

    429 Pattern Hlfp., n.d. Bust same as Ceylon type, 1815. ℞ Same as Ionian Isl., 1819. Proof ; not brilliant ; dark olive. Rare.   1

430 1799 Far. and Hlfp., 1806, $\frac{1}{4}$, $\frac{1}{2}$ and 1 Penny ; 1807 do. Good to unc.   8

431 Geo. IV. Third Farthing, 1827. Unc. Half Farthing, 1830. V. good. Both uncommon.   2

432 Farthings, 1821 to '30, excepting '24, with two types of '26 ; Hlfp. and Pence, 1825, '26, '27. Good to unc. 4 of last.   16

433 Wm. IV. Third Farthing, 1835 ; Half do., 1837. Both fine ; the latter rare.   2

434 Farthings, Halfp. and Pence, various dates, 1831–37. Mostly good to fine. Halfp. of 1837. Unc., red.   11

435 Victoria. Quarter Farthing, 1839 ; Third do., 1844, and new type, 1866 ; half do., 1842. Good to unc.   4

436 Quarter Farthings, 1852, '53 ; Third do., 1868–85 (5) ; Half do., 1843–54 (7). Fine to unc. Most of last.   14

437 Farthings, 1838–57 (17) ; Halfpence, 1838–59 (15) ; Pence, 1841–59 (12). Mostly good to fine ; some unc.   44

438 Farthings, 1860–87 (22) ; Halfpence, 1860–88 (24) ; Pence, 1860–87 (25). The new bronze coinage instituted in 1860. Mostly good to fine ; some in mint state.   71

/ **439** **Scotland.** Chas. I, Chas. II, Wm. and Mary. Fair and good, with a Bawbee of Chas. II. Nearly fine ; a scarce lot.   11

440 **Ireland.** Eliz. 1601 and '02, Halfp. and Farthings of Jas. I and Chas. I (2 var.) Fair to fine.   5

441 Chas. II. Halfp., 1680, '81 (2 var.), '82, '83. Jas. II. Hlfp., 1685, '86. Wm. and Mary. Hlfp., 1692, '93, '94. Fair to fine ; some uncommon.   10

442 Jas. II. 1689 Gun money. Jan., VI, XII, XXX Pence ; Feb., XII ; July, VI ; Aug., XII, XXX ; Sept., XII, XXX ; Oct., XII, XXX ; Nov., XII. Mostly good to fine.   12

443 Varieties of those in preceding lot. VI (3), XII (8), XXX (2). Mostly good to fine, 1 holed.   13

444 A Half Crown (XXX) of Aug., with date (in legend) directly
beneath the month. Obv. good, rev. fair.   1
A variety valued highly by the late Chas. H. Wright, but one that he did not own.

445 1690 March, XXX ; April, XII ; May, XII, XXX ; June, XII,
XXX, and Crown, with king mtd. " Hibernia." The king
setd (struck after exile, by his followers). Good to fine.   8

446 Varieties of those in the preceding lot. Fair to fine. Small
XII (3) ; large XXX (1); small XXX (5), and Crown (1).   10

447 Geo. II. Farthing, 1760 ; Halfp., 1731–60 (7). Geo. III.
Farthings, 1806 ; Halfp., 1766–82 (5), 1805, also Penny,
1805. Geo. IV. Halfp., 1823 ; Penny, 1822. Fair, good,
and fine, equally portioned.   19

448 1760 VOCE POPULI Halfpence. Bust r. ℞ Hibernia setd l.
9 varieties, including P. before bust and the same letter below (2 var.) Fair to fine.   9

449 Duplicates of English, Scotch and Irish coins in the preceding
lots. Includes some very scarce pieces, among which are 8
Scotch, Gun money of James II, Elizabeth Hlfp., 1601, etc.
Only 16 of the present century. Many good ; a few fine.   80

Seventeenth Century Tokens.

The Series described by Boyne.

450 Issues by Mayors, Aldermen, Overseers, Bailiffs, etc., of Towns
and Boroughs. Andover, Bath, Beccles, Boston, Coventry,
Dorchester, Dover, Marlborough, Peterburg (octagonal),
Romsey (¼ and ½d.), Shaftesbury, Walton, etc. A descrip-
tion of the last shows much of the general character of
the series :—BY ˙ THE ˙ MAIOR ˙ AND ˙ ALDERMEN * In field,
a wool-pack separates 16 | 69. ℞ THIS ˙ FARTHING ˙ WILL ˙
BE ˙ OWNED * In field (script), *in | Walton | vnder | edge*
Mostly very good ; 1 holed.   35

451 Others issued by shopkeepers, taverns, etc ; various towns ;
many quaint and interesting devices and types. There are
representations of human figures, animals, arms, etc. This
and the two following lots are believed to form a collection,
and they are separated as uniformly as possible as to variety of size (each lot contains one octagonal), type and
condition, which latter will be found to be very good.   60

452 Another.   61
453 Another.   64
454 The holed, culled from the preceding (11), together with
       the duplicates and varieties, among which are 19 of
       Bristol.   43
455 *Lead Tokens.* GOD SAVE THE QUENE. A rose, crowned, sep-
       arates E — R. ℞ Double-headed eagle. Very fair. 21.
       S. H. 1753 (retrograde), good, 25, and others, probably
       later, and some, location unknown. Mostly good ; 1 holed.
       16 to 25.   12

Eighteenth Century Tokens (mostly Irish).

Early.

456 1731 I. Maculla, 20 Shil. Justice between columns. 29. Jas.
       Adair, B. Mena (Ballemena), 2P. A rabbit *r.* 23. Edwd.
       Smyth, Twopence. Unicorn crest *l.* 23. Last two undated.
       V. fair to good. All scarce or rare.   3
457 1731 Edinburgh Token. A castle, date below. ℞ D G linked,
       Smith 40 pl. 14. Fine, rare. Lead, 17 x 19.   1
458 1734 Wm. Ringland, Belfast, 1 and 2 Pence. Dove flying.
       "Good tidings." Good and fine, rare. 21, 24.   2
459 Others of Ringland, with 2 | P before dove. One has plain
       rev. Both fair. 25. Also, Thos. Fisher, Twopence. A
       kingfisher stdg *l.* Fine. 23. None common.   3
460 1735 Clifton, CS. L. Walton. ℞ 1 · K, CS. 17 | 35 Hugh
       Magarrah, Belfast, 1736, 2P. Wolf *l.* "Fierce and strong"
       (poor). 1761 John McCully, Newtown. A cask sep. 2 — P.
       Good. 22 to 25.   4
461 1760 Thomas | Jordan | and Co. | Three Pence. ℞ Good-
       mans-Fields Brewhouse. A bear *l.* chained. Holed, as
       issued. Brass. V. good and rare. 31. Also, Covent Gar-
       den — Pitt | 1762 Fine. 35.   2
462 Others, undated. Curwen, Hensingham, Manor of Munster
       (John Rice), Landsale, Porter | Nelson. ℞ A ship sailing,
       Qveeneborough. Good, some rare. 26 to 28.   6
463 Monogram. ℞ Arms, and ℞ Griffon, another, arms, ℞ Large
       4, etc. Ak. pl. 7, No. 5, etc., includes 1 octagonal. Fair to
       fine. 23 to 33.   6

The series of ENGLISH TOKENS described by *JAMES CONDER* in 1798, including issues of the 20 years preceding. The collection here submitted approaches nearer to completeness than any before offered for sale in this country, and I feel it is safe to add, that no one here ever drew so many together. The nucleus of the collection was made up from the Mickley, Nichols, and Doughty cabinets; another and important source, was aid rendered by English dealers, who were supplied with lists of numbers wanted. The eccentric spelling on the pieces has been followed, usually without comment.

The Conder references are indicated by figures ; the bracketed figure [1] refers to page, the others to the particular number on the page.

PENNIES.

464 Anglesey. Paris Mine Co., 1784–89. A Druid's head. [1] 1, 2, 3, [2] 4 to 9. Good to unc., with 2 proofs. — 9

465 Others, 1788–90, and n.d. [2] 10, 11, [3] 12 to 19, except 14. Mostly unc. or proof. — 9

466 Dundee, 1797, Town House; Cambridge, Christ College Gate, King's College Chapel. [11] 3, [19] 2, 4. Unc. and proof; all rare. — 3

467 Cambridge. Trinity College Gate, [19] 6. Chesterton, near Camb., [20] 7. Chester Castle and East Gate; all with "British Penny" reverse. [22] 1, 2. Unc. and proof. All rare. — 4

468 Bernard's Castle, Durham; Sunderland, Iron Bridge. 2 differing. [32] 1, 2, 3. V. fine and unc. All rare. — 3

469 Gloucester. Cathedral, "St. Mary de Crypt," St. Mary de Lode, the new County Gaol, etc., by *Kempson ;* 2 are by *Ottley,* and in white metal ; both rare. [37] 1 to 7. Proofs. — 7

470 Gosport, 1798. Drum and flags, T. Wood, salesman, etc.; Netley Abbey, Hants. [40] 1, 2. Both rare. — 2

471 Hereford. Prancing bull *l.,* by *Milton ;* another with June 3, 1796. [45] 1, 3. Unc. Halsall, [55] 1. Fine. — 3

472 Loch-Leven, 1797. Castle. ℞ Girl treading clothes in tub. [53] 1. Proof. Lancaster Castle. ℞ Lancaster Bridge, [55] 1. In white metal. V. fine ; both rare. — 2

473 Middlesex. Westminster Hall ; Banqueting House, White-Hall ; Queen's Coll. Gate, Camb. All by *Jacobs.* [68] 1, 2, 3. Unc. ; all rare. — 3

474 — Swan swimming, [68] 1. Hackney Church, [69] 1. Unc. and proof ; both rare. — 2

475   Kew Palace, Middlesex, 1797. Unc., rare. Halls, three quad-
      rupeds. Unc. The deformed figure of Sir Jeffery Dunstan.
      Fine. [69] 8, 10, 11.   3

476   *Kempson's.* Guild Hall, Mansion House, and " back front " of
      Somerset House, [70] 15, 16, 17. Unc. and proof ; all rare.   3

477   — Bank of England, St. Bartholomew's Hospital, Bethlem
      (sic) Hospital, [70] 18, 19, 20. Unc. and proof ; rare.   3

478   — Carleton House, Chelsea, Christ Church Hospital, [70] 21,
      [71] 22, 23. Fine to proof ; rare.   3

479   — St. Paul's Church, Foundling Hospital, St. George's Hos-
      pital, [71] 24, 25, 26. Unc. and proof ; rare.   3

480   — Goldsmiths' Hall, Greenwich Hosp., Guy's Hosp., [71] 27,
      28, 29. Unc., rare.   3

481   — St. James's, Ironmongers' Alms House, [71] 30, 31. St.
      Luke's Hospital, [72] 32. V. fine to unc. ; rare.   3

482   — Middlesex Hosp., Montague House, Monument, [72] 33,
      34, 35. Unc., rare.   3

483   — Ordnance Office, Royal Exchange, St. Thomas's Hospital,
      [72] 36, 37, 38. V. fine and unc.   3

484   — Trinity Arms House, London Bridge, [72] 39, 40. West-
      minster Bridge, [73] 42. Unc.   3

485   — Black-Friars' Bridge, Aldgate, Aldersgate, and Bishops-
      gate, [73] 43, 44, 45, 46. Unc. and mostly bright.   4

486   — Bridge Gate, Cripple Gate, Ludgate, [73] 47, 48, 49.
      Moorgate, Newgate, [74] 50, 51. Unc.   5

487   House of Commons, Goldsmiths' Hall, and New Excise Office,
      [74] 53, 54, 56. Unc. and proof.   3

488   Pantheon, an original brass cast. Geo. III visited St. Paul's,
      another, different, and in white metal ; also, " Attended Di-
      vine Service," and Low's Grand Hotel, 1774, [75] 57, 58,
      59, 62, 63. Fine to unc.   5

489   *Skidmore's.* Addington Place, Carisbrook Castle, and Cowes
      Castle (both Isle of Wight), [76] 65, 66, 67. Very fine to
      proof.   3

490   — Dulwich College ; Bishop of London's seat at Fulham ;
      seat of David Garrick, Esq. ; House of Lords, [76] 68, 69,
      70, 71. Unc.   4

491   — Fort George. Part of Isleworth, St. Paul's School, [77] 72,
      73, 74. Unc.   3

O C **492** *Skidmore's.* Rivalx Abbey, Sion House (near Brentford), Smallpox Hospital, [77] 75, 76, 77. Unc.   3

'' () **493** — South Sea House, Lord Stormont's, [77] 78, 80. West Clandon Place, Horne Tooke, Esq. ℞ Sessions House ; Young, Dealer in Coins, [78] 81, 83. Unc.   5

ɔ **494** London and Westminster, 1797. Bank of England, Drury Lane Theatre, King's Theatre, Haymarket, [78] 84, 85, 86. Unc. and proof.   3

495 — Trinity House, City of London Lying-in Hosp., [78] 87, 88. Lambeth Palace, Sessions House, Old Bailey, [79] 89, 90. Unc.   4

496 — Treasury, St. James's Park, Tower of London, Westminster Abbey, Albion Mill, [79] 91, 92, 94, 95. Unc. and proof.   4

497 — St. Paul's School, Brewers' Hall, Cordwainers' Hall, Dyers' Hall, [80] 97, 99, 100, 102. Unc. and proof.   4

⹁ , **498** — Fishmongers' Hall, Grocers' Hall, [80] 103, 104. Ironmongers' Hall, Leadenhall, [81] 106, 107. Unc. and proof.   4

499 — Merchant Taylors (sic) Hall, Skinners' Hall, Stationers' Hall, Late Surgeons' Hall, [81] 109, 111, 112, 113. Unc.   4

500 — Tallow Chandlers' Hall, [81] 114. Vintners' Hall, Wax Chandlers' Hall, [82] 115, 116. Unc. and proof.   3

, ɔ **501** Norwich Castle, Wroxham (3 Pence), [117] 2, 3. Unc.   2

502 Yarmouth. Female setd, holds scroll. ℞ Britannia setd, receives curiosities from representatives from Asia, Africa and America, [117] 4. Unc., very rare.   1

503 Nottinghamshire. Newstead Abbey. ℞ British · Penny · — 1797 In field, T S in script, [124] 1. Proof, very rare.   1

504 Sherborne . Castle . — Oxfordshire, [125] 1. Dudmaston — Shropshire ; Ludlow Castle, Salop, [128] 1, 2. Proofs.   3

505 Bath. Abbey Church, Botanic Garden, M. Lambe & Son, [130] 1, 2, 3. Glastonbury Abbey, [131] 10. Fine to proof.   4

506 Bungay. An ancient fortress. "Bungay Halfpenny," with edge inscribed "Double Token" etc. Bungay Tower, Suffolk, Bury. Chas. Marquis Cornwallis, [141] 1, 2, 3, 4, 5. Hoxne, [142] 6. Unc.   6

507 Ipswich. Cardinal Wolsey. Bust *l.* ℞ An ancient gateway, above, Jaˢ Conder Ipswich 1795 ; below, Wolʸˢ Gate. Another with rev., Payable | at | Conder's | etc. 1796 [142] 8, 9. Unc., very rare.   2

508 Town Hall Ips!! — Formerly St. Mildreds | Church. View of an ancient bldg. ℞ Conders Ipswich Penny — 1797 etc. Another with same rev., one having obv. same as those in last lot, the other a gateway, same as first rev. in last lot. [142] 10, 11, 12. Unc., very rare.   3

509 Woodbridge. Thos. Sekford, [142] 13. Godstone Tower, Surrey; Guilford Tower, Lambeth Palace, [147] 1, 2, 3. Unc.   4

510 Lambeth. Man stdg, smoking, holds mug and keg of beer, [147] 4. Unc., v. rare.   1

511 Battle Abbey, Sussex, [151] 1. Warwickshire. P. K. in script. ℞ Ancient fortress. The Birmingham Poet. T. W. in script, linked. ℞ arms, [160] 1, 2, 3. Unc.   4

512 Coventry. St. Michael's Church, [160] 4. Kendal, T. Hall. Kendal Castle, [175] 2, 3. Worcestershire. M. S. in script, linked, [177] 1. Unc.   4

513 Dudley. Part of Dudley Priory, 1797; dif. view of Dudley Priory; the chapel in Dudley Castle; Tower of Dudley Castle, all issued by E. Davies, Nail Factor, [177] 2, 3, 4, 5. Unc. and proof.   4

514 Evesham Tower and Church, Payable by T T (in script) June · 6 · 1796 · [178] 6. Bowes Castle, Yorkshire; Fountains' Abbey; Ruins of Gisborough Abbey, [180] 2, 3, 4. Unc. and proof.   4

515 Sheffield. Constitutional Soc'y. ℞ 1792, 4 flags draped, one inscribed AMERICA, BRITAIN on shield, [181] 5 (edge plain). V. fine.   1

Not Local.

515a British. Geo. III, 1789, bust by *Droz.* ℞ Serpent, burning altar. Obv. and rev. silvered, edge gilded, [199] 2. V. fine.   1

516 Geo. III, 1789, bust *l.*; another, head *r.*, [200] 3, 5. The Rev. Caleb Evans, bust *l.*; "Glory be thine intrepid Fox;" The Right Hon. Chas. Jas. Fox, [202] 16, 17, 18, 19. Very fine to unc. All in white metal, and rare.   5

517 Geo. III, 1797, Penny. A bronzed proof of the regular coinage from the Soho mint, [200] 7.   1

518 Georgivs III . D. G. Rex. Bust *r.* ℞ T. G. in script, British Penny, 1797, [200] 8. French folly in building rafts; Cabbage Society Purim, 1796, [201] 10, 11. Unc.   3

519 ADMIRAL DUNCAN. Bust facing. ℞ Struck | in honor of | etc.
in 13 lines, [201] 14. Unc., very rare.   1

520 THO. HOWARD · COM · DE · EFFINGHAM etc. Head *l.* by *Milton*,
edge inscribed in raised letters, [201] 15 (also illustrated on
Conder's plate III). Unc., v. rare.   1

521 Fox. Resistless Speaker, etc., [202] 17, in both copper and
brass. Fine. Admiral Gardner. ℞ "Some of the Foxes
tricks on a Westminster Pole 1796," [203] 21. Unc. and v.
rare.   3

522 GREATHEADS — WRONG | HEADS — RIGHT | HEADS — MEETING
AT WARWICK | MAY 31 1797 3 men in cart drawn by ass,
etc. ℞ AS IF | FROM TEMPLE | BAR etc. in 8 lines, [203] 22.
V. fine, rare. White metal.   1

523 Thos. Hardy facing bust "Not Guilty," [203] 23. Johnson,
pugilist, "Masonic Penny"; Perrins, pugilist, [205] 29, 32,
35. Promissory. Lion sleeping at mouth of cave; Monument, [206] 39, 40. Unc.   6

524 Busts of Hardy, Tooke and Thelwall conjoined *r.*; John Howard, Adm'l Earl Howe, Selina, Coun'ss Dow'r of Hunting-
don, [204] 24, 25, 25, 26, 28. Thos. Paine, [205] 34. Wm.
Pitt, [206] 36. Wm. III. ℞ "Britons | never | will be |
slaves"; Rev. Wm. Romaine, [207] 43, 44. All with bust
and in white metal, a rare assemblage. Two are fair, others
fine to unc.   8

525 Vincent Lunardi, bust *l.*, "First aerial traveller in England,"
[205] 31. Unc. Jos. Priestley, bust *r.*, by *Hancock.* ℞
Philosophical appliances, [206] 38. Fine; both rare.   2

526 Revolution. Britannia setd. ℞ Bust of Wm. III, 1688
below, without legend, [206] 41. Lion *l.*, rev. as last, with
wreath around border; Rev. W. Romaine, [207] 42, 45.   3

527 The Penny of Scotland (1 oz.), 1797; Adam Smith, LL. D.,
etc. Bzd proof. Sedition. Monster flying. ℞ "Nourished
to torment"; snake in grass, [207] 46, 47. Fine; both rare. 2

528 Sheridan, "Resistless wit," etc.; "Am I not a man and a
brother"; Lord Thurlow; "When | we forget | him | may
God forget | us"; another, with bust of Pitt on rev.; John
Wesley, with 3 different revs. (1 fair); Doctor Willis, [208]
48, 49, 50, 51, 53, [209] 55, 57, 59, 60. A rare group, in
white metal. Fine to unc.   8

529 Geo. Whitefield. A good soldier, etc. (Betts, 526), [209] 59.
Hackney.   Sheffield Constitutional Society.   ℞ Hackney
Church, [263] 3.   Revolution.   Lion, same as in 526.   ℞
Same as first in 515, [264] 5.   Fine and unc.   3

Appendix.

530 Anglesey, [309] * 14. "Dundee Penny," 1798, bust of Adm'l
Duncan, [311] * 3.   Gloucester.   The High Cross, St.
John's Church, [313] * 1, 2.   Proofs.   4

531 St. Mary de Lode, White Friars, [313] * 3, * 7.   Proofs.
Birmingham Work House, 2 Shil. and 6d., 1788, [320] *
1. Fine. Brass.   3

532 T. Gordon, London.   Poker, tongs, shovel and fender.   ℞
T. G. in script. "British Penny—1797" in relief, on raised
border, [315] * 9. Unc., v. rare.   1

533 BRITISH COMMERCIAL PENNY.   Bust of George III *r.*   ℞
BRITANNIA. Female setd *l.* on cannon ptd *r.*   Ex. 1797,
Spink 746, Mont. 25. [320] * 6. A bronzed proof; very
rare.   1

Pennies, not found in Conder.

534 1787, Anglesey, 1790, do., also Macclesfield, with bust of Roe.
The last 2 bzd proofs.   3

535 1794, Lancaster Bridge. ℞ Lancaster Castle (Æ gilt), very
fine.   Dublin.   To prevent the abuse of charity in the con-
sumption of whiskey, etc., in 9 lines.   ℞ Value | One Penny
etc. Good.   Norwich Loyal Military Ass'n.   Unc.   3

536 1798, Bⁿ Jacob | Auctioneer | etc., Birmingham   ℞ Merchant
behind counter.   Unc., red.   Matthew Young, Dealer in
Coins and Medals.   Setd figure, with city arms, before St.
Paul's, Promissory Penny Token on edge in relief.   A bzd
proof.   2

537 The arms of Gloucester, by *Ottley.*   ℞ St. John's Church, St.
Nicholas' Church, high cross taken down.   V. fine; about
unc.   In white metal.   3

HALFPENNIES.

538 Anglesey. A Druid.   ℞ · P. M Cº in script.   1788 (4), 1789
(2), 1790, 1791 (2).   [4] 20, 21, 22, 23, 24, 25, 27, 29, 31.
All unc. or proof.   9

539 Others, with varying revs., cipher, Vulcan, woolpack and arms.
[5] 32, 34, 35, [6] 37, 38, 39, 40, [8] 57, 58, 59. John Wilkinson " Wilkison," 1787–93. [6] 43, 44, [7] 46, 47, 48, 49,
50, 51. Good to fine. 18
540 Others, with Druid's head ; 3 have P. M. Co. in monogram ;
1 reads " Halfpeny (sic) on Demand." [7] 52, 53, [8] 55,
56. Unc. and proof. 4
541 Washington, President. Bust *l*. ℞ Halfpenny above ship *r.*,
below, 1793. Good. 1
542 Aberdeen, [10] 1, v. rare. Dundee, ship at key, rev. tower,
[11] 4. " Crooms." Infirmary, Glass Works, Dudhope Castle, St. Andrew's Church, [12] 5, 6, 7, 8, 9. All unc. or
proof. 7
543 Forfar. View of the town, 1797, [12] 10. Montrose, [13] 11,
12. Flintwick Church, [15] 1. Windsor, a stag *r.* beneath
tree, rev. Windsor | Halfpenny | Token | 1795, [16] 1.
Skidmores Edge. V. rare, unc. 5
544 " Amersham Token," 1797, Aylesbury. Justice setd and bust,
[17] 1, 2, 6. Chesham, [18] 7. Cambridge, [20] 8, 9. Caer-
marthen, [21] 1. Beeston Castle (rare), Chester, Macclesfield, [22] 3, 4, 5, [23] 6, 7, 8. Fine to unc.; most of last. 13
545 Macclesfield, Chas. Roe's bust (5), [23] 9, 10, 11, 12, [24] 14.
Others, including William Pitt, P. M., [24] 15, 16, 18.
Cornwall Co., Falmouth, Penryn, [26] 1, 2, 3. Good to
proof. 11
546 Buxton. Stags support arms. ℞ A building in semicircle,
below, CRESCENT | 1796 Edge, " Buxton Token." Marked
varieties of obv. [28] 2, 3. Unc., very rare. 2
547 Exeter, Plymouth, [29] 1, 2, 5. Poole, Bayly's and Allen's.
℞ Poole | Halfpenny | Payable · in | Dorsetshire | and ·
Devon | 1797 Very rare. [31], 1, 3. Unc. and proof. 5
548 Sherborne. P. P. & W. in script ; another with bldg, rev.
Preter | Pew & Whitty | Bankers | Sherborne | Dorset |
1796 *Rare.* [31] 5, 6. So. Shields, [32] 4. Braintree,
Chelmsford, Colchester, [33] 2, 3, 4. Very fine and unc. ;
most of best. 6
549 Sunderland. Wearmouth Bridge, erected 1796, [32] 6. Dun-
mow. A flitch of bacon, [34] 5. Unc. The latter has
crack in planchet ; both rare. 2

l.5r **550** Epping Forest, 1796 (last two figures reversed). VALUE ONE
SHILLING ℞ A stag and tree, [34] 6. Unc., very rare. 1

551 Hornchurch, Maldon, Warley, [34] 7, 8, 9, 10. Glamorgan,
Swansea, [36] 1, 2. Brimscomb Port, Gloucester, [38] 10,
12. Newent [39] 14. Unc. 9

552 Woodford, 1796 Token, Essex. Compass, wheel, saw and
axe, [35] 11. Rare. Badminton. A beggar receiving alms,
[38] 9. Basingstoke Canal Shilling, by John Pinkerton,
[40] 3. Unc. 3

553 Emsworth, [40] 4, [41] 5, 6, 7, 8. Gosport, Isle of Wight,
Halfpenny, by Robt. Bird Wilkins, [41] 9, 10, 11, 12.
Petersfield [42], 14, 15, 16. Very fine to unc.; some
scarce. 12

554 Lyndhurst. Geo.(rgivs) III Rex · ℞ Visited | Lyndhurst |
Lymington | etc., 1789, in 7 lines, [42] 13. Hereford.
Honiatts and T. Gortons, the latter with portrait in profile *l.*
[45] 4, 5. Fine and very fine ; all very rare. 3

32 **555** Portsmouth, [42] 17, 18, 19, [43] 20, 22 (the last "Viscount
Jarvis"). Portsea, [43] 23, 24, 25. Southampton. Bust *l.*
2, both fine work ; bust *r.* 4, one fine work, [43] 26, [44] 27,
29, 30, 31, 32. Mostly fine to unc. ; some rare. 14

556 St. Albans, 1796, Stortford, [46] 1, 2. Inverness, [47] 1, 2, 3
(and another dated 1796). Unc. and proof ; a choice lot. 6

557 Appledore, Benenden, Brookland, Canterbury, Deal, Deptford,
Dimchurch, Dover ; the last with bust of Wm. Pitt, [48] 1,
2, 3, 4, 5, [49] 6, 8, 9, 10, 11, 12. Mostly unc. and
proof. 11

558 DOVER TOKEN. View of castle. ℞ "Dedicated to collectors
of Provincial Coins, 1795." A military trophy within wrth.
[50] 14. Unc., very rare. 1

559 Feversham, Goudhurst, Hawkhurst, Hyth, Lamberhurst, Rom-
ney, Sandwich, Staplehurst, Tenterden, [50] 15, 17, 18, [51]
20, 21, 22, 23, [52] 26, 27, 28, 29. Unc. ; some very uncommon. 11

560 Folkstone, 1796. Ships at Key ; a proof, very rare, [50] 16.
Maidstone, [51] 24, 25. Both unc. and rare. 3

561 Gatehouse, 1793, [54], 1. Lancaster, complete, 4 to 18, excepting 16, with bust of John of Gaunt, Danl. Eccleston and
John Wilkinson. Mostly very fine ; some unc. 15

562 Lancaster. "E Pluribus Unum." Pyramid of 13 stars, last
   with initial letter of State, K. for *Kentucky*, at top. Lettered
   edge. [57] 16. V. fine, light olive ; rare.   1
563 Liverpool, 1791–95. Ship, rev. arms. John of Gaunt, Earl
   Howe, etc. [57] 19, 21, 22, 23, [58] 24, 25, 26, 30, 31, [59]
   33, 36, 37. Mostly very good and fine.   12
564 Manchester, [59] 38, 39, 40, [60] 43. Rochdale, complete
   (5). Glasgow, complete (5) ; includes the rare John Howard rev. Fine to unc. ; most of best.   14
565 Lincoln, Sleaford (both scarce), Spalding, Wainfleet, (63) 1,
   2, 3, 4, 5. Fine to unc.   5
566 Edinburgh. Archibald, seedsman, both varieties, New Uni-
   versity, 1797, [64] 1, 2, 4. Fine to unc. ; all rare.   3
567 Edinburgh. Halfpenny, 1796, above, Register Office, by
   Wright, [64] 3. Unc., red, very rare.   1
568 Turk's bust *l.*, 2 var., 1 smoking. A highlander in full dress ;
   all payable at Campbell's snuffshop, St. Andrew's street,
   [64] 6, [65] 7, 8. Unc. ; 2 are rare.   3
569 St. Andrew with his cross, 1790, '91, '92 and '96 (the last
   rare), Harrison, [65] 9 to 14, [66] 15, 16, 17. Fine to unc. ;
   most of last.   9
570 R. Sanderson & Co.—No. 17 South Bridge Street. Rose and
   thistle entwined, crown above. ℞ Sells | all kinds of |
   Woollen & Linnen (sic) | etc., in 8 lines, [66] 18. Brass.
   Fine, *very* rare. Another with eagle on serpent, having same
   legends, rev. from *same* die, not mentioned by Conder.
   Very fine, and doubtless quite as rare as its companion.   2
571 Leith, [66] 19, 20, 21. Hendon, London, Allen's, Bebbing-
   ton's, Birchell's, [84] 123, 125, [85] 131, 133, 134. V. fine
   to uncirculated.   8
572 Bethnal Green, St. Matthew's Church, Bow, Moses Stone, 1797,
   Chelsea, sailor with wooden leg, [83] 117, 118, 119. Very
   fine (1) and unc. All rare.   3
573 Hackney Church, different views ; Geo. Butler, Oilman. Paint-
   pot, cask and brushes crossed, [83] 120, 121, 122. All unc.
   and rare.   3
574 Hornsey, church behind trees. London, Anderson's P. A. in
   script monogram. Bayly's, a crocodile *r.* [84] 124, 126,
   129. All unc. and rare.   3

575   Black Friars, Biggar's (both rare), [85] 130, 132. Clark's
"Washington Grate Cent" (scarce), [86] 137. V. fine.   3

576   Carter's, Chambers', Corresponding Soc'y (2, includes the rare
one with bust of Prince of Wales), Coventry Street, David-
son's, Dennis's, Eaton's, Foundling Fields, Fowler's, Guest's,
[85] 135, 136, [86] 138, 139, 141, 142, [87] 143, 145, 147,
149, [88] 151.   Very fine and unc.   11

577   Corresponding Soc'y. "Liberty · and · not · slavery." Man
hanging on gibbet.   Fine, very rare.   Dodd's, with head of
Handel.   Unc., rare.   [86] 140, [87] 144.   2

578   Foster's, Hall's (complete).   White negress, Jeffery Dunstan,
and various animals, [87] 146, [88] 152 to 157.   None common.   Fine and unc.   7

579   Franklin Press, 1794.   V. fine, scarce.   Hancock, Umbrella
Maker & Dealer in Provincial Coins.   An umbrella opened.
Another, a shop front, small umbrella above.   Both unc.
and rare.   [88] 150, [89] 158, 159.   3

580   Hatfield's, [89] 160, Kelly's, Lackington's, bust facing, 3 var.,
bust r., 2 var., [90] 165 to 170.   Mostly unc.   7

581   Heslop's.   A man and monkey each standing on one foot, with
the other raised to head.   "Can you do so?"   James's
"Royal male tiger," 1796.   Ibberson's, St. George killing
dragon, [89] 161, 162, 163.   The last 2 rare.   V. fine to unc.   3

582   London and Middlesex.   Bust of Shakespeare, Geo., Prince
of Wales, John of Gaunt, John Wilkinson, etc.; Lyceum,
Mail Coach, Meynott's and Moore's, [90] 172, [91] 173, 174,
175, 177 to 181, [92] 182, 183, 184, 185, 187.   Very fine to
unc.; some rare.   14

583   Neeton's, "A Saracen's head."   Newgate Prison, 3 var.   Geo.
III visited St. Paul's.   Pidcock's, complete; lion, eagle,
dbl-headed cow, antelope, elephant, Royal male tiger, etc.
[93] 188, 189, 190, 191, 193, 194, 195, [94] 196 to 199.   V.
fine to unc., most of the best; several rare.   11

584   Prattent's London Commercial Token, 1796; Presbury's, with
bust of Queen Elizabeth; Ratley's, man yawning, holding a
framed picture, [94] 200, 201, 202.   All unc. and rare.   3

585   Richardson's, Rupert Street; Salter's, Schooling's, Shackel-
ton's, Sims, with head of Garrick, Skidmore's "Register
Stove," [94] 203, [95] 204 to 208.   V. fine to unc.   8

586 Skidmore's. A guillotine, Liberty cap on pole, LIBERTAS above, 1796 below ; a man skating in HYDE PARK, [96] 212, 215, 216. All unc. and very rare.   3

Skidmore's Churches and Gates.

587 St. Mary, Abchurch Lane ; St. Mary's, Aldermanbury ; St. Ann's and St. Botolph, Aldersgate ; St. Bartholomew, the Great and the Less ; St. Michael, Basinghall Street ; St. Mary-at-Hill, Billingsgate, [97] 218 to 225. Unc.; all rare.   8

588 St. Botolph, St. Ethelburge and Great St. Helen's, Bishops- gate ; St. Ann's, Black Fryars ; St. Botolph, Botolph Lane ; St. Mary, Bow Lane ; St. Mildred's, Bread Street; St. Swithin, Cannon St., [98] 226 to 233. Unc. ; all rare.   8

589 St. Lawrence, Cateaton Street ; St. Mary le Bow, Cheapside ; St. James, Clerkenwell (4 var.) ; St. Stephen's, Coleman Street, [99] 234 to 240. Unc.; all rare.   7

590 St. Michael, College Hill and Cornhill (west view); St. Paul's, Covent Garden (2 var.) ; St. Giles, Cripplegate ; Alhallows, Crutched Fryers ; St. James's, Dukes-Place, [100] 241, 242, 244 to 248. Unc.; all rare.   7

591 St. Catharine, Coleman Street ; St. Mary Magdalen and St. Nicholas, Old Fish Street ; St. Bride and St. Dunstan's, Fleet Street ; St. Matthew's, Friday Street; St. James, Gar- lick Hith, [101] 250 to 256. Unc.; all rare.   7

592 St. Giles's-in-the-Fields ; St. Bennet, Gracechurch Street ; St. George's, Hanover Square ; St. Andrew's, Holborn, and Leadenhall Street ; Allhallows, Lombard Street, [102] 257, 258, 259, 262, 263, 264. Unc.; all rare.   6

593 St. Edmond the King, St. Mary, Woolworth, both Lombard Street ; St. Magnus, London Bridge ; St. Alphage, London Wall ; St. Margaret's, Lothbury ; St. Mary's, Love Lane ; St. Martin's, Ludgate (2 var.) ; St. Trinity, Minories, [103] 265 to 273. Unc.; all rare.   9

594 St. Olave's, Old Jewry ; St. Luke's, Old Street ; St. Bennett's, Paul's Wharf (2 var.) ; St. Mildred's-in-the-Poultry ; St. Michael, Queenhith ; St. George's, Queen Sq. ; St. Paul's, Shadwell ; St. Sepulchre, Snow Hill [104] 274 to 282. Unc.; all rare.   9

/.ſ ℓ **595** Shoreditch Church; St. Ann's, Soho; Spitalfields Church; St. Clement's, Strand; Alhallows, Thames Street; St. Martin-Out-Wick, Threadneedle Street; Chapel in the Tower; St. Margaret Pattens, Little Tower Street; St. Stephen's, Walbrook [105] 283 to 291. Unc.; all rare. 9

596 St. John's, Wapping; St. Mary's, White Chappel; St. Alban's and St. Michael, both Wood Street; Aldgate, Aldersgate, Bishopsgate, Bridge-Gate, Saint John's Gate, [106] 292 to 296, 298 to 301. Unc.; all rare. 9

597 Cripplegate, Ludgate, Moorgate, Newgate, Temple Bar, Robert Orchard, London Token, 1797, [107] 302, 304, 306, 307, 308, 310. Unc.; all rare, the last especially so. 6

/ **598** *Spence's.* An ass loaded with two pairs of panniers. "A Blue Coat Boy," "A Bridewell Boy," British Liberty Displayed, [107] 311, [108] 312, 313, 314. Unc.; all rare. 4

599 — Little Turnstile Halfp. A dog, "Much gratitude brings servitude." R! H? C. J. Fox. R̸ "We also are the people." Soldier and citizen shaking hands, [108] 315, 316, 318. Unc.; all rare. 3

600 — Head of Fox. R̸ "We were born free and will never die slaves." Lord George Gordon, also a similar one, with legend. R̸ Sessions-House,—Old-Baily [108] 319, [109] 320, 321. Unc.; all rare. 3

601 — A Marine Society Boy, D. Mendoza. R̸ Two men boxing. Cain killing Abel. R̸ Two men dancing around a fire. "The end of oppression." [109] 332, 333, 334. Unc.; all rare. 3

/ **602** — A pig. Man sitting in prison gnawing a bone. R̸ A cat. "I among slaves enjoy my liberty." A highlander. "The gallant garb of Scotland." [109] 325, 327, 328. Unc.; the last two rare. 3

603 — "A true hearted sailor." A Spaniard stdg. Head of Spence. R̸ An American Indian stdg. "If rents I once consent to pay," etc. [110] 329, 330, 331. Unc.; very rare. 3

604 — John Thelwall. Horne Tooke, Esq. A Turk standing, and United Token, 1796. [110] 332, 333, 335, 336. Unc.; all rare. 4

605 — A Deserted Village. A collegian standing. Spittle's, with St. Paul's (2 vars.) Stinton's, Grasshopper. [111] 337 to 341. Unc.; 2 are rare. 5

606 Sumner's. The head of a wild man, facing. "From the land of Jesso," etc. ℞ R. S. in script, Dealer in curiosities, etc., 1797. [111] 342. Unc. This piece has frequently been referred to as "the rarest Conder."　1
607 P. of W. elected Grand Master. Long live the King. ℞ "Payable at John Whitfields" (Conder adds "in London"). A pair of scales (very rare). Williams, Portcullis, John Howard. [111] 343, [112] 345, 348, 349. Fine to unc.　4
608 Westminster. St. James's Church, Whitehall Gate. Paddington, New Church. [112] 351, [113] 352, 353. Unc.; all rare.　3
609 Stepney Church, Stoke Newington Church, Willsdon Church. [113] 354, 355, 356. Unc.; all rare.　3
610 Abergavenny. Jas. Powell, Wine and Brandy Merchant. Another, with different rev. for Monmouth. [116] 1, 2. Unc., rare.　2
611 Aylesham. Blofield (complete, includes the Talbot, A. & L. rev.), Buxton. [118] 5 to 11. Fine to unc. Mostly uncommon to rare.　7
612 Norwich (complete, excepting 21), including Norwich Cathedral, with bust of Handel on rev. Another, with bust in armor; both rare. [119] 12 to 19, [120] 20, 22 to 28, [121] 29. Fine to unc.　17
613 Yarmouth, [121] 30. Northampton, [122] 1. Nottingham, [124] 2. Banbury, [125] 1. Perth, [127] 1, 3, 4, 5. Colebrook-Dale, Shrewsbury, [128] 4, 5, [129] 6, 7, 8. Fine to unc. Some are rare, and especially the last, with Lackington's rev., and Shrewsbury, with Bishop on rev.　13
614 Yarmouth. Same type as the Penny No. 4, [121] 32. Unc., very rare. Perth, 1797. ℞ Water-mill and trees. [127] 2. Unc., rare.　2
615 Newcastle. Coaly Tyne, 1797. A barge sailing. North Shields. Cart unloading into ship at end of pier. [123] 3, 4. Unc.; both very rare.　2
616 Somerset. Yeomanry Cavalry, 1796. ℞ Three light horsemen, mtd. Bath. [132] 12, to [134] 26. Fine to unc. Some are rare, notably one of Gye's and Lamb & Son of 1795.　16

617 Bath. All Saints' Chapel, Cross Bath Pump Room, Free
Church, Free School. [134] 29, 32, 33, 34. Unc. and proof.
All rare.   4

618 — Gen'l Hospital, Kensington Chapel, St. Mary's Chapel (2
var.), Private Baths, Stall St. [134] 35, 36, [135] 37, 38, 40.
2 good, others unc. and proof. All rare.   5

619 — Interior of New Pump Room, principal entrance ; Walcot
Turnpike Token, 1796; "No Trust," etc. [135] 41 to 45,
[136] 46, 47, 48. Fine to unc. Several rare, and especially
so are the last two.   8

620 Bridgewater (2 types). Bristol. "Gold, silver or copper I
.can command, Value One Halfpenny upon demand." Another, Two men in conversation, etc. [136] 49, 50, 52, 53,
[137] 54 to 58. Fine to unc. Several rare, the last piece
uncommonly so.   9

621 Dunkirk and Dunkikre, [137] 59, 60. Leek (3 var.), "Litchfield Token," with bust of Dr. Johnson, Stafford, [139] 1 to
5. Beccles, Blything, Bungay (5 var., 1794, '95), '96, [143]
14, 15, 17, 18, 19, [144] 20, 21. Fine to unc. ; most of last.
Four are rare.   14

622 "Tipton Halfpenny." North view of a church. ℞ Payable
in Staffordshire, 1797. An anchor. [139] 6. Unc. ; uncommonly rare.   1

623 Bury. P. Deck's, Goer's, Abbey Gate, "Going agoing," Ha-
verhill (2 var.), Hoxne (2 var.), Ipswich, including 2 of Conder's own, 1 with bust of Cardinal Wolsey. [144] 22 to 27,
[145] 28 to 33. Mostly unc. The last is rare, others scarce.   12

624 Lowestoft, [145] 34. Sudbury [146] 35, 36. Battersea, Croydon, Guildford, [148] 6, 7, 9, 14, 15, [149] 16. The last
(a Druid's head,) with Croydon, is rare. Good to unc.   9

625 Lambeth. Same type as the Penny. [149] 17. Brighton.
Officer stdg before camp. ℞ Soldiers besieging a city. Another with ships at sea, military trophy below. [151] 6,
[152] 7. Unc. ; all very rare.   3

626 Bermondsey. St. Mary Magdalen's, Bermondsey Priory, [148]
10, 11. Rotherhite, St. Mary's ; Southwark, Christ Church,
St. John's, St. Olave's, St. Saviour's and St. Thomas's ; all
churches, by *Jacobs*. [149] 18 to 23. Unc. ; all rare. The
last two are of the highest degree.   8

627 Battel, Brighton, [151] 2, 3, 4, 5. Chichester, with bust of
Queen Elizabeth ; Eastbourn, Frant, Grimstead, [152] 9 to
13. Hastings, Northian (complete), [153] 14, 15, 17 to 20.
Fine to unc. The choicest prevail. 2 rare, some others
very uncommon.   15

628 Horsham. Bust, "Long live the King." ℞ M. Pintosh, etc.,
1791 ; edge, "Skidmore Holborn London." [153] 16 (edge
milled). Rye. G. Bennett, scales, chests of tea, etc., 1796.
Winchelsea. [154] 21, 22. Unc. The first 2 are very
rare.   3

629 North Wales. Brutus Sextus, Celestine II, Pope, etc. [155]
1, 2, 3, 5, 6, 7, [156] 8 to 12, 14, 15, 16, 18. Fair (1 holed)
to unc. The Druid heads are fine to unc., with some very
rare.   15

630 Others, [157] 19, 20, 22 to 29, [158] 32, 35, 36, 38 to 43.
Includes "Georgeivs Washington." Good to fine ; all of the
"Bad Halfpence" style, like those in the preceding lot,
excepting the Druids.   20

631 Warkwickshire. Birmingham, 7 to 18, excepting 17. Busts of
Shakespeare, Gen'l Elliot, setd female, etc. Good to very
fine ; some very uncommon.   13

632 Gen'l Elliot. Bust l. ℞ P. S. in script. [162] 19. Boy stdg
leaning on screw. ℞ Three men hanging on a gibbet.
Birm. Poorhouse. "Payable there." [163] 23, 25. Unc. ;
all rare.   3

633 Others, Arms, Dr. Johnson (scarce), Donald & Co., John Wilkenson (scarce). [163] 20, 22, 24, 27. Bisset's Museum,
John Howard. [164] 30, 35. Good to fine.   6

634 "Union Mill Birmingham," 1796 (no date given by Conder).
℞ Wreath formed of wheat ears. A plain field in which
107 stamped incuse. [163] 26. Good, extremely rare.   1

635 John Wilkison. Bust r. ℞ Halfpenny 1794, etc. [164] 29.
Oak tree and ships at sea. Wm. Hallen, with bust and
without. [164] 32, 33, 34. V. fine to unc. Rare and very
rare.   4

636 Kempson's. Bust of Geo. III. Ashted Chapel, Barracks, St.
Bartholomew's Chapel, Blue School, Blue Coat Charity
School, New Brass Works, New Brewery, [165] 37 to 44.
Unc. ; all rare.   8

637 *Kempson's.* Free School, Gen'l Hospital, Hotel, St. John's
Chapel, St. Martin's Church, [165] 45 to 49. St. Mary's
Chapel, the Old Meeting and Oldmeeting, [166] 50, 51, 52.
Unc.; all rare.   8

638 — New Meeting, Meeting, Paradise St., Navigation Office,
New Jerusalem Temple, Old Cross St. Paul's Chapel, St.
Philip's Church, Soho Manufactory, [166] 53 to 60. Unc.;
all rare.   8

639 — Birm. Theatre, Welsh Cross, [166] 62. Birm. Workhouse,
Library and Coining Press, [167] 63, 64, 65. Unc.; all rare
but one.   5

640 Coventry. Lady Godiva nude on horseback, 1792, '93, '94,
'95, [167] 66 to 70, [168] 71. Fine to unc.; as a lot and
series, rare.   6

641 CIVITAS COVENTRIÆ Setd female. ℞ "Peeping Tom" look-
ing from window of house. MEMORIÆ Edge inscribed in
raised letters, "Payable by Tho : Sharp" etc. [168] 73. A
bzd proof. Among the greatest rarities in the series and a
very celebrated token.   1

642 Bablake Hospital (2 var., 1 with bust of Handel), the Barracks, Remains of Cathedral, [168] 74 to 77, [169] 79. Unc.
(1) and bzd proof; all rare.   5

643 Coventry Cross, County Hall, Drapers' Hall, Ford's Hospital
(2 var., 1 has bust of Handel), [169] 81, 83 to 86. Bzd
proofs; all rare.   5

644 Free School (dif. views), [169] 87, 89. Grey Friars Gate and
Steeple (2 var. of last), [170] 90, 92, 93. Unc. (1) and bzd
proof; all rare.   5

645 St. John's Church (2 var.), St. Mary Hall, Mill Lane Gate,
Spon Gate, [170] 94, 95, 96, 98, 100. Unc. (1) and bzd
proof; all rare.   5

646 Spon Gate (with a different rev.), Trinity Church, White
Friars Gate (two varieties) and White Friars — Founded,
[171] 101, 102, 104, 105, 106. Unc. (1) and bzd proof; all
rare.   5

647 Meriden. Token, 1796. "Prize for Archery." Unc. Nuneaton Arms and Lady Godiva. V. fine. [171] 108, 110.
Both rare.   2

648 Nuneaton; John Wilkinson; Stratford, bust of Shakespeare;
Willey, bust of John Wilkinson. Varieties, 1787 to 1795;
includes the rare "Wilkenson." [172] 111, 112, 113, 115 to
118, [173] 119 to 127, [174] 128. Good to unc., and 1 bzd
proof. 17

649 Willey. John Wilkinson, Iron Master. ℞ Man working at a
forge, window in the building. [172] 114. Very fine, very
rare. 1

650 Kendall (complete), [175] 4 to 7. Wiltshire, Devizes, Holt,
Salisbury, [176] 1, 2, 3, 4, 6, 7. Unc.; all mostly bright;
some are rare. 10

651 Dudley Token. ℞ Shepherd reclining beneath tree. Hagley.
A man angling in brook. [178] 7, 10. Unc.; both v. rare. 2

652 Stourbridge. Brirley · Hill Token. North view of a church.
℞ R. Astin, Malster, etc. [178] 12. Unc.; extremely rare. 1

653 Worcester. [179] 13, 14, 15. All brass and scolloped edges.
Fine to unc.; 2 very uncommon. Bedal. Perspective view
of street, 1792. ℞ Jas. Metcalf. Beverly. J. Green, Pawn-
broker, 1796. Unc.; both rare. 5

Note. — The remainder of the Conder series will be sold in Part II, which
will take place early in the fall.

Period of 1810–15.

654 Barnsley, n.d. V. fine, light olive. Bath, 1811. Fleece and
arms. Both unc. Bewicke Main Colliery, 1811. V. fine,
light olive. Pennies. 4

655 Bilston, 1811. Bust *r.* and *l.* Pennies, 2 var. each. 1812,
bust *r.* Halfp. and Penny; also Sam'l Fereday Penny.
Good to fine. 7

656 Birmingham, 1812. Union Copper Co. (2 die var.) Workhouse, 1812, '13, 14 (poor). Birmingham and Neath, 1811.
All Pennies. Birmingham and Swansea, 1811, Halfp. (3 die
var.) Penny, 1812, "Copper Token — One Penny" A
rose. Good to fine. 11

657 Birmingham. Three Pence, 1813. Some light nicks, most on
arms side, also a few edge dents, otherwise fine; a medium
olive. Not common in any condition; very rare when so
choice. 1

658 Bristol, 1811. Bust *r.* Penny, arms ; Halfp. and Penny (both unc.) ; Pat. Sheathing Nail Mfy. ; Far., Halfp. (2 die var.) and Penny, ship on obv. ; also a variety of the Penny, Payable by T. Guppy, Bristol and So. Wales, 1811, Penny. Good to v. fine.   9

659 Carmarthen, 1813 ; Cheltingham, 1812 ; "Cornish Penny," 1811 ; Scorrier House and County, 1812, " Penny Piece "; also Scorrier House, rev. bust and P. of W. crest, " Cornish Penny," n.d. ; Cornish Mount, all Pennies. Mostly fine.   9

660 Culross . Wester . Main . Colliery. Farthing (very good) and Halfp. without date (slightly clipped, but fine). Both very rare.   2

661 Doncaster, 1812 ; Dudley and Birm., 1811 ; Flint Lead Wks., 1813 (2 die var.) ; Glasgow, Phoenix Iron Wks. ; Glastonbury (no date), "Pro Patria et Avalonia," Halesowen, 1813 ; Hull Lead Wks., 1812, (6, 5 are die varieties), all Pennies ; 1812, Lead Wks., Halfp. Good to very fine.   14

662 Litchfield (Lemmonsly Mill) ; Liverpool Docks (holed) ; London, Mail Coach ; Mihell's " Caravan Office," all without date ; Romanis, 1814 ; Nantiglo, 1811 ; Newark, 1811 (2 die var.) ; Newcastle, 1813. Halfp. 3, Pennies 6. Good to fine.   9

663 Norwich, 1811, Halfp. (2) and Penny, 1815, Overseers of the Poor (poor), and Twopence, n.d. (nicked). Good to fine.   5

664 Nottingham, 1812, '13 (3 var.) ; Sedbury, Sheffield, 1811, Halfp. ; 1812, Halfp. (2), Penny ; 1813, Penny (poor). Gd. to fine.   10

665 Priestfield Furnaces, 1811, Penny (2 varying revs.) and Twopence. Very choice in condition and color. Rare.   3

666 Sheffield, Overseers of the Poor, 1812, '13 ; Phoenix Iron Works, 1813 ; Hobson, Swansey and So. Wales, 1813 ; Staffordshire, 1811 (2 var. of rev.) ; Baylis, Pottery, 1813, all Pennies ; 1814, Halfp. and Penny. Good to fine.   11

667 Stockton, 1813 ; Taunton, n.d. ; Tavistock, 1811 (2 die var.) ; Tunstead and Happing, 1812 ; Worcester, 1811. Pennies, 6 ; Halfp., 2. Good to v. fine.   8

668 Walsall, 1811, Pennies (4 die var.) and Halfp. ; Walthamstow, Pennies, 1812 (3 die var.), 1813 ; Withymoor, 1813 ; Wiveliscombe, n.d., both Pennies. Good to fine.   11

669 Worcester, 1813, John Knapp, Junior. Farthing, Halfp. and
Penny. Fine to unc. 3

Later Period.

670 Birmingham (2), Ewanrigg Colliery, Hoxton, Liverpool Zoolo-
gical Gardens, Lancashire, 3ᵈ 1827 (2, one CS. J. H., not
mentioned by Sharp), Manchester, Norwich, 1849, Rosher-
ville Botanical Garden. All Halfpenny size. Good to fine. 10

671 London. (Halfpennies, unless otherwise stated.) Bake, Jno.
Clark & Co., 1854 (Victoria's head), Court Gazette, Dutton,
Henry (Coin Dealer), Kendall's, 25 Drury Lane, etc.,
"One Pint" (size 52), Prof. Holloway 1857 Halfp., 1858
do. and Penny, Sweet Scents (Æ and brass), and Mr. Till's
(Coin Dealer) Farthing and Halfp. 1834. Fine to unc. 13

672 Others : Temperance Halfp. 1840, Royal Colosseum (2 sizes),
"The wise son of a pious father" etc. Good to fine. 9

673 Irish Penny Tokens. 1800, bust Geo. III ; 1802, Charleville
Forest (18 Pence, a bzd proof), W. F. B. & Co. ; 1805, '13,
Coleraine, Dublin, Strabane ; 1815, '20, '58, Cloughjordan ;
1863, Coal-island, issued by W(ilson) ; 1866, Armagh Flax
Spinning Mill L(aurel) H(ill) Residence of Proprietor.
Mostly good. 12

674 1802, Charleville, as last, but a gilt proof ; 1815, St. Patrick
Apostle ; 1816, "Wellington & Erin go bragh" by *I. Parkes*,
℞ Stephens' card (Sandham classed with Canadians) ; 1818,
"Luke xx : chap." etc., bust *r.* and *l.* Good to fine ; all un-
common. 5

675 Halfpence. 1801, "The Union"; 1804, 3 var. ; 1805, "St.
Patrick Apostle," also "Apos "; 1813, '14 (only fair, but
rare), '19, '20, '34. Some fine. 11

676 Farthings by merchants, mostly time of Victoria, none late.
Belfast 5, Cork 4, Donegall Place, Dublin, 9, Galway 3,
Limerick 2, Skibbereen 2, Tralee. Good to fine. 27

MAN AND CHANNEL ISLANDS.

677 **Isle of Man.** 1709 Halfp. and Penny. Eagle on cap. ℞
Three legs joined. Fine original casts ; rare. 2

678 1733 Penny. 1758 Halfp. and Penny, A. D. in script, linked
and cwnd. 1786 Geo. III, same values. One fair, others
very good. 5

679 1798 Geo. III, Halfp. 1811 Penny, Atlas carrying the world
     (rev. silvered, probably by Dr. Clay), also Bank Halfp.
     1813 Geo. III, Halfp. and Penny. Good to fine.   5
680 1811 Penny. View of Peel Castle. Douglas Bank Token.
     About good ; very rare.   1
681 1830 "God save the King." Halfp. and Penny, both in brass
     (2 var.) and copper. 1831 Pro bono publico. Fair to fine.   6
682 1839 Victoria, Farthing, Halfp. and Penny. V. fine to unc. ;
     1 partly bright.   3
683 **Guernesey.** 1 Double, 1830, '85, '89 ; 2 do., 1868, '85, '89 ;
     4 do., 1830, '64, '68, '85, '89 ; 8 do., 1834, '58, '64, '68,
     '85, '89. Fine to unc. 1885 and '89 Form complete, unc.
     sets.   17
684 **States of Jersey.** Victoria. 1841 $\frac{1}{52}$, $\frac{1}{26}$ Shilling. Unc.,
     the latter bright red.   2
685 Others, various, 1841–88 $\frac{1}{48}$, $\frac{1}{36}$, $\frac{1}{24}$, $\frac{1}{13}$ and $\frac{1}{12}$ Shilling, repre-
     senting 3 types. Good to unc.   19

SCANDINAVIA.

686 **Norway.** Fred. VI, 1809 1 and 4 Skillings ; 1810 2 Sk. (2
     var.). Chas. XIII, 1 Sk. 1816. Chas. XIV, 1 Sk. ; 1819,
     '20, '31, '32, '33, 2 Sk. ; 1822, '24, '27, '28, '31 to 34. Good
     to fine.   19
687 Various late issues, 1839–89 $\frac{1}{2}$ and 1 Sk., 1, 2 and 5 Ore.
     Fine to unc.   15
688 **Sweden.** John III, various, 1 and 2 Ore, 1573 to 1592, and
     1 Mark, 1592. Sigismund, 1597 1 Ore. Some are for
     Stockholm. All struck as base coins, though now appearing
     like copper. Mostly fine. 18 to 31.   9
689 John III, 1691 4 and 8 Ore. 18 x 19 and 21 x 22. Good and
     v. good, rare.   2
690 Duplicates of Stockholm 2 Ore, and 2 of the square 8 Ore.
     Good.   3
691 Gust. II, Adolph., 1615 $\frac{1}{2}$ Ore (base) ; 1 Fyrk, 1–F, 17 x 21,
     and $\frac{1}{2}$ Ore, 23 x 23. Dates do not show on last two, other-
     wise good ; all rare.   3
692 1625 Half Ore ; 1626 1 Ore. Poor and fair ; date shows upon
     2. 18 x 22 to 27 x 27.   5

693   1625 1 Ore, G — A — R and 3 crowns. ℞ Arrows crossed,
     1 — OR Good, rare. 34 x 35.   1

694   1626 1 Ore, as last ; obv. not well centered, but type and date
     intact. Rev. faultless. Fine, rare. 28 x 30.   1

695   1626 2 as last, varying dies. V. good and nearly fine, rare.
     24 x 29 and 26 x 30.   2

696   1626 2 Ore. Fasces sep. z — ÖR, date below. ℞ G A R — S
     with crown above. Very good and very rare. 39 x 39.   1

697   1626 Arms. ℞ Eagle. 1 Ore for Arboga. 1627 1 Ore.
     Arms. ℞ Eagle, and ℞ Arrows. Fine to about good ; rare.
     40 to 42.   3

698   1627 1 "Fyrck" and 1 Ore, the latter with arms, *rev.* eagle.
     Both rare. Good. 24, 34.   2

699   1628 1 Ore for Arboga. 1629 another for Nyköping. Fair,
     rare. 41, 28.   2

700   1628 ½ and 1 Ore. 1629, '30, '31, 1 Ore. Fair, 1 very good.
     35 to 42.   5

701   1628, '29 Arms, ℞ Arms ; '30 (?) ℞ Griffon. Very good to
     fine.   3

702   1630 ½ and 1 Ore. Cwnd arms. ℞ Arrows crossed. Fine.
     33, 40.   2

703   1632 1 Creutzer. Arms. ℞ Arrows crossed. 1 : CR-EUTZ.
     Nearly fine, rare. 37.   1

704   Christine. 1634 ¼ Ore ; 1650 1 do. About fine. 30, 47.   2

705   1635, '36, '37, '41, '44, '48, ¼ Ore ; 1645, '46, '48, 1 do. Mostly
     very good ; 1 holed.   9

706   1645, '48, '51, '52, 1 Ore. One on octagonal planchet, 50 x 52,
     others, size 48. Good to fine.   4

707   Chas. X, Gust., 1656 ¼ Ore. Chas. XI, 1661 1 Ore ; 1664
     2 do., both K : M. : 1669 1 do., S : M : All fine. 29, 34,
     42, 47.   4

708   Chas. X, ¼ Ore, 1657, '58, '59 ; Chas. XI, ⅛ Ore, S. M., 1668,
     '71–74, '76, '77, '81, '82, '83, '86. Sizes 26 to 29, with 7
     small coins for Riga, by Christine, Chas. X, Gust., etc.
     Mostly very good.   21

709   Chas. XI, ⅛ and 1 Ore, S. M. ; ½ and 2 do., K : M : 1663 to
     1677. Good to fine.   4

710   1663, '65, 2 Ore, K. M., size 41 ; 1673, '75, '76, '78, '79, '85,
     '86 1 Ore, S : M : 47. Mostly very good.   9

710a 1670 $\frac{1}{8}$ Ore, S. M. Two impressions (obv. and rev.) on copper
plate, 1$\frac{1}{2}$ and 2$\frac{1}{2}$ inches ; probably the original method of
striking, after which they were cut out in circular form. V.
fine.   1

711   Chas. XII, $\frac{1}{8}$ Ore, 1707–18 (2 types), and Baron de Gortz
Dalers, 1715, '16, '17, '18 (6), '19. Mars, Mercury, etc.,
complete, also laur. head *r*. (sometimes called de Gortz).
℞ Mercury stdg. Mostly v. good.   16

712   A set of the de Gortz Dalers, 11 types, with die varieties of 10,
and all varying from those in preceding lot. Many fine,
some unc.   23

713   1715 $\frac{1}{2}$ Daler, Plate Money. XII between two C's linked and
cwnd, sep. date stamped in the four corners. $\frac{1}{2}$ | DALER |
S : M in centre within lozenge-shaped frame. Fine, very
rare. 4 x 4$\frac{1}{2}$ inches.   1

714   Ulrica Eleonora, 1 Ore, 1719 (2 var.), 1720. Fred. I, $\frac{1}{2}$, 1
and 2 Ore, S. M., and 1 do. K. M., dates 1720–50. Good
to fine.   8

715   Fred. I, 1721 $\frac{1}{2}$ Ore, S. M., and various 1 and 2 Ore, do.
1730–50 with 1 do. K. M. (3 dates), sizes 23 (4), 30 (12),
34 (5). Mostly very good.   21

716   Plate Money. 1722 $\frac{1}{2}$ | DALER | SILF : MYNT in centre within
circle. F R S cwnd, date below, in 4 corners. Clipped
on each corner, possibly as issued. Fine. 3$\frac{7}{8}$ x 4$\frac{1}{4}$
inches.   1

717   1723 1 Daler. Type as last, corners clipped. Fine, rare.
5$\frac{1}{4}$ x 5$\frac{1}{4}$.   1

718   1727 2 Daler. Quite as the preceding in every respect. Rare.
6$\frac{1}{4}$ x 7 in.   1

719   1732 4 Daler. Like the preceding. Fine, rare ; corners un-
clipped. 9$\frac{3}{8}$ x 9$\frac{3}{8}$.   1

720   Adolf Fred., 1 Ore, K. M., and 1 and 2 do. S. M., 1764–68 ;
Gust. III, 1 Ore, K. M., and 1 and 2 Ore, S. M., 1772–78
(each a dif. type). Good to fine.   6

721   1 and 2 Ore, S. M., each of year 1751, '58, '59, '60, '61 and
'63, and 2 do. 1762, '65, '67 ; also 1 Ore, Gust. III, 1778.
Good.   16

722   Plate Money. 1758 $\frac{1}{2}$ Daler, A F R S in the 4 corners, cwnd.
Fine. 3$\frac{3}{8}$ x 4$\frac{1}{4}$ inches.   1

723 Gust. IV, Adolf, 1794 ½ Skilling, July 9th, 1799 ¼ and ½ Sk., Globe type; 1802 $\frac{1}{12}$, ¼, ½ and 1 Sk., G. A. IV cwnd; Chas. XIII, $\frac{1}{12}$, ¼, ½ and 1 Sk., 1812–17. Good to very fine.   11

724 Other dates and die var., $\frac{1}{12}$ to 1 Skil., 1800–17. Good to fine.   22

725 Chas. XIV, John, $\frac{1}{12}$, ⅙, ¼, ½ and 1 Sk. XIV within large C, cwnd, 1819–30. Bust r. 1832 ⅙, ¼, ½ and 1 Sk. (a rare set). Good to fine.   9

726 Other dates and die varieties of last, ⅙ to 1 Sk., including the ¼ Sk. 1833, bust type. Good to fine.   18

727 1836 ⅙, ⅓ Sk., XIV within large C; ⅔, 1 and 2 Sk. Bust; v. fine to unc. Oscar I, ⅙, ⅓ Sk., O. cwnd; ⅔, 1, 2 and 4 Sk., with head r. Unc., red. Very desirable; difficult to equal.   11

728 Differing dates of Chas. XIV, John. ⅙, ⅓, ⅔, 1 and 2 Skillings, 1835–43. Mostly good to fine.   24

729 Oscar I, 1858 ½, 1, 2 and 5 Ore (last 3 hd l.); Chas. XV, 1861–63, and Oscar II, 1873 Types and values same (excepting ½ Ore, Os. II); O. II, cwnd, 1889 1, 2 and 5 Ore. Mostly unc.; 12 bright or partly so.   14

730 Differing dates. Os. I, ⅙, ⅓, ⅔, 1, 2 and 4 Sk. and ½, 1, 2 and 5 Ore. Many fine; some unc.   38

731 Others: Chas. XV, 1, 2 and 5 Ore, and Oscar II (O. II cwnd), same values. Mostly fine; some bright red, others partly so.   51

732 Tokens. Avesta, Höganäs, Kopparberg, Sald, Trollhattan, Wiken, etc. 1674, 1715, 1719, 1723, and some undated, but none late. All numbered in envelopes, according to Scharp. The lot includes several sets. Mostly good to fine. An interesting and rare collection.   30

733 Others, differing, of Kopparberg, etc., not named. 1759, 1762, 1763, 1765, 1768, 1790, 1791, and some undated, but all early, including medalets or jetons of Gustavus I, Chas. (X), Gustavus, 1660, and Chas. XII, all with bust. Good to very fine, 1 holed, some rare.   19

734 Others of later period, Christinehamn (1), Goteberg (3), and Stockholm; the remainder, Bridge, Ferry, Omnibus, Hotel and Store Tokens for various values, enveloped and numbered by Scharp. Mostly fine and in brass; some oval and octagon.   28

735 Some very good duplicates of Sweden, and mostly early, including Stockholm, de Gortz Dalers, Kopparberg and other Tokens, but chiefly coins. 49

736 **Denmark.** Chris. V. 1670–99 C. 5, cwnd sep. II — S(killing). D(ankse). ℞ Plain, 25 x 25 ; also, same design for 8 Skillings, 29 x 33. Good, very rare. 2

These Necessity Pieces were issued May 1st, 1677, by the Danish Genl. Meerheim, when besieging the city of Christianstadt,

737 Chris. V, Fred. IV, Chris. VI, Fred. V, Chris. VII, Fred. VI, Chris. VIII, Fred. VII and Chris. IX, 1693 to 1881. Good to fine, some unc., red ; a very complete line of types and values. 34

738 Die varieties and differing dates. Seven reigns from Chris. V, 1696, to Chris. IX, 1875. 31 pcs. Schleswig-Holstein, 1787, Dreiling and Sechsling ; 1850, same values ; 1851, Sechsl., and a small coin of Eric of Pomerania, 1396–1439, for Odense. 37

739 **Low Countries.** Artois, Battenburg, Bomel, Bronkhurst, Cambray (4 early), Campen, Culemburg, 1590, Daventer, East Friesland, Friesland, Flanders, Gelderland, Ghent, Gorcum, Groningen ; Mytes, Liards, Doits, etc., 15th to 17th centuries. Mostly fair to good ; some rare. 34

740 Brabant. Chas. V, 1543 (with his head), to M. Theresa, and later, to include Revolution, 1790. Mytes, Liards, etc., mostly with portrait. Many good, with some very choice. 45

741 Gelderland, 1752–94 (16), Hanau, Phil. II (2), Holland, Phil. II, 1576 to 1780 (including the large dbl Doit of 1739, 13) ; Leyden, 1573 ; Maestricht, Necessity, 1579 ; Phil. II, 1590, etc. (6). Doits, Sols, etc. Mostly good. 41

742 Nymwegen (2), Overyssel (8), Reckheim, Ruremond (2), Stevensweert, Tournay (4), etc., 16th to 18th century. Fair to v. good. 24

743 Utrecht, 1723–92 (18), Zeeland, 1579 to 1794 (18), Zierikzee, 1585, Zwolle, (16)39, '96. Liards, Doits, etc. Fair to good. 39

744 The Kingdom of the Netherlands. W (for William), cwnd. ℞ Arms. ½ Cent, 1822–76 (17) ; Cent, 1821–77 (18). Some varieties in mint marks. Also, ½, 1 and 2½ Cents of the new coinage of 1877 (10). Mostly fine ; some unc. 45

745 Tokens, etc. Amsterdam, 8 | W undated and R. B. 1789
(both lead) ; Antwerp, 1605 ; Coomans Gilde, 1745 ; Holland Prison Tokens ; Middleburg, 1660, etc., including 3
neatly engraved pcs. (1752, '73 and '97). Good to fine ;
several rare.   19
746 Lille, Parish of St. Cath., Maestricht, 1676 ; St. Bartholomew
Church, Middleburg, 1737, Load of peat for the poor, etc.,
including a beautiful modern jeton of Tournay. Good to
unc., 1 holed ; mostly rare.   7

HISTORICAL JETONS OF HOLLAND.

16th and 17th Centuries, dates from about 1550 to 1697 all numbered according to
Van Loon and in square pasteboard coin holders. Condition is generally good, a few
are poor and 4 holed ; there are also a small number of die varieties.

747 Vol. I.   Various from page 7 to 218.   30
748 — Page 223 to 309.   30
749 — Page 309 to 405.   30
750 — Page 408 to 471.   34
751 — Page 474 to 556.   33
752 Vol. II.   Various from page 5 to 41.   25
753 — Page 43 to 130.   25
754 — Page 142 to 324.   25
755 — Page 327 to 511.   30
756 Vol. III. Various from page 5 to 318 (18). Vol. IV, p.
253 (1).   19
757 Belgium. Leopold I and II. Differing dates of 1, 2, 5
and 10 Centimes (but 2 of the 10c). Mostly good to
fine.   48
758 Alost 1833 1 and 5 Ctms. Gand 1833 1, 5 and 25 do. Reckheim 1841 5 and 25 do. St. Bernard 1833 1, 5 and
25 do. "Monnaie Fictive." Good to unc. All very uncommon.   10
759 Luxemburg 1757 (2), '59 (2), '75, '83, '86, '89, '90 and others
later, 1854 to '70, also 2 unofficial Essais of 1889. Good to
unc. Scarce lot.   17
760 Liege. Ernst of Bavaria 1584 to John Theo. 1752, with
Mereaux of Chapters. Sous, Liards, etc. Mostly fair to
good.   23

/o 761 **France.** Chas. IX, 1514, and X. Hy. III, dates 1579–83.
Henry IV (6), 1603–10. Louis XIII (20), 17 dates, 1612–43.
Louis XIV (15, including 1 of 1655–56, with bust on both
sides, in beautiful condition), 1647–1658. Chiefly Double
Tournois. Also some base of prior reigns (3), and an early
Gaulish pc. holed. Size 20. Fair to good.   49

/ / 762 Louis XV, 1719 Sou. Very fine, light olive. 1720 Half Sou
Unc. red. Boy head *r*. Two gems.   2

763 1768 Sou. 1769 Half Sou. Old head, unc., light olive. Ex-
ceptional specimens.   2

764 Liard, Half Sou, and Sou, large head, 1766–71. Not as well
executed as the preceding, in fact rather crude. V. fine to
unc.   3

765 Various dates and mints. Liards, Half Sous and Sous. Louis
XV and XVI, 1720 to 1791. Mostly fair to good.   24

766 Louis XVI. 3 and 6 Deniers in copper, good. 12 Den. and
2 Sous in brass, v. fine, the latter with an exceptionally
strong obv., 1791–92.   4

767 Various mints, 1791–92. 6 and 12 Deniers and 2 Sous. Fair
to fine, mostly good.   19

768 Republic. 1793, ½, 1 and 2 Sous. Tablet. ℞ Scales. Fair
and v. good. Also 5 Ctms. and Decime year 4 with head
of Liberty. Fine.   5

769 Others of varying mints and years. 1 Sou (2), 2 do. (4). Fair
to abt. good. Also Liberty head. 1 Ctme. (3), 5 do. (8),
1 of the small type). Mostly good, some approaching
fine.   17

770 1 Decime, years 5 to 8. Various mints, including the rare
Geneva. Also 2 Decimes year 4. Many very good.   12

771 Nap. I. 1808 5 Ctms., large N. 1814–15 Decime, Louis
XVIII. 1814–15 Decime. All Strasburg mint. Also, Ctme.
pcs. of the 2nd Republic, 1848, '49, '50, '51. 1 poor, others
mostly fine.   9

772 Nap. III. Various mints and symbols of directors and mas-
ters of the mint. 1, 2 and 5 Centimes, 1853–57 ; 10 do.,
1852–57. Bare head *l.* Many fine, some uncirculated,
red.   77

773 Laureated head, 1 and 2 Centimes, 1861–62 ; 5 and 10 do.,
1861–65. Condition as last.   31

774 3rd Republic. 1870 Liberty head *l.*, from old die, by *Dupre.*
R⁷ Liberte Egalite — Fraternite. In field, 10 | Centimes |
1870. Strasburg mint. Unc., rare.   1

775 Head of Concord *l.* 1, 2, 5 and 10 Ctms., different dates, all
Paris mint but three. Good to unc.   18

776 *Patterns and private issues.* 1791 "Caisse de Bonne Foi,"
3 Sous, slight die varieties, by *Theve.* Another with "Foy"
for 2 Sous, 6 Den. Monneron Bros., 2 and 5 Sols, the latter with soldiers in line swearing to the Constitution. 1792
5 Sols, same design, with differing revs. Good to fine,
some scarce. 24 to 40.   7

777 1792 Monneron. 2 and 5 Sols, sim. to preceding, with "Revolution Française" on rev. Proofs ; the latter bronzed.   2

778 1792 Others by Monneron. 1, 2 (2 var. of rev.) and 5 Sols.
Hercules breaking fasces. "La fin du despotisme" V.
fine ; slight edge defect on 5 Sols. A rare set.   4

779 1792 Fasces, Liberty setd, and other patriotic devices, by
Michael Brezin ; size of 2 Sols (1), 5 do. (5). Fine ; none
common, some rare.   6

780 1792 Genius of France, ins. tablet. R⁷ PIECE | D'ESSAI Æ,
27. 1793 Similar, brass. 31. Liberty setd, facing. "La
loi des François" R⁷ ESSAI | AN — II Also, 2 Sols, tablet.
R⁷ Wreath and scales, in lead, bzd. V. fine to perfect.   4

781a 1793 "Régénération Française" 5 Decimes. Brass. 35.
Year 3. *Dupre's* Liberty head. R⁷ 25 . | CENTIMES | L'AN
3. Below, a small facing head (Brussells ?) 24. Also 1 |
Franc. | 50 | Centimes bet. fasces ; incuse design, without
date. 30. V. fine to perfect ; rare.   3

781 1796 Caisse d'Escompte. Lion within wreath. 1797 A cock
strutting *l.* ; below, "Vigilance" Both fine ; size 31. Another, n.d., Ant · Laur · Lavoisier · Head *r.* Unc. 26.
Rare.   3

782 1816 Nap. II. 1, 3 and 10 Ctms. and Half Franc. Head *l.*
R⁷ Value within wrth, date below. About perfect ; bright red.   4

783 Louis XVIII, n.d. Head *l.* below ESSAI R⁷ Cwnd shld bet.
branches. Chas. X, 1824. Crown above fleurs de lis, both
for 2 Fcs. Chas. X. Head *l.* 10 Ctms. in brass. Louis
Phil., 1843. 2 Ctms. brass. 1847, 2 do. a dif. design. V.
fine to perfect, some rare.   5

784 1848 Republic. 10 Ctms. 3 differing designs. Good to unc.
Also 1 Gascon for Aquitaine. A remarkable design, abt.
perfect, size 40.   4

785 1870 "G^t de la defense Nationale" a balloon. ℞ Republic
Française. Within wreath, 10. 1889 1, 2 and 4 Ctms.
Mercury and female; holed through centre same as Congos.
Dijon. 5 Ctms. n.d., line of silver through planchet. Fine
to perfect, none common.   5

786 Tokens and cards. Dixain, 1791 (2 sizes, 3 metals). Anzin,
Script mon., and 1 dated 1820, 30 Sous. Another for 12
Sous. All Miners' Tokens. Good to fine, some rare. 25 to
34.   6

787 Bread Tokens of St. Andre des Arco and St. Barthélemi (2,
one for meat). Free school of Design, with Paris shop
cards. Good to fine, none common.   13

788 Baronial, Ecclesiastical, etc. Bellai, Bouillon, Chateau-Renaux,
Dombes, Lorraine, Montbelliard, Nevers, Pfalzburg and
Lixheim, Roussillon, etc. Deniers, Doubles, Liards, etc.
16th to 18th Century. Mostly good.   47

789 Jetons. *Copper*. With head right. Revs. have historical allu-
sions; dates, 1677 to 1708, and some undated. Many good
to fine.   38

790 Others with *bust* right, 17 have dates, 1652-83. Mostly very
good.   45

791 Louis XV. Head *r.* (5), bust *r.* (7). All dated between
1717 and 1757. Good to fine.   12

792 Cardinal Richelieu, Chomel (poor), F. de Harlay, L. Alex. de
Bourbon, Mar. Theresa, and 5 others, with bust of Louis
XIV and consort, etc. Fair to good.   15

793 *In brass.* Henry IV (2), Louis XIII (8), Louis XIV (14), all
with bust; Louis XIV and consort (2). Many good.   26

794 Louis XIV, with his head *r.* Many good.   27

795 Louis XV, bust or head *l.* (9); do. *r.* (10). Many good.   19

796 Louis XVI, bust or head *r.* and *l.* (22); Nap. I (13, one in
copper); Louis XVIII (2), etc. Many good, 2 holed; all
ordinary work.   40

797 *With arms.* 1556 to 1792. A varied lot. One reads SORIN |
1712 Another has seven men holding sphere. Fair to very
good.   34

798 Others in copper, 1557 to 1754, and without date. Fair to
very good, 2 holed.   23
799 Personal Jetons, 1582, '85, etc., to 1729. Arms, stdg figures,
ships, etc. ; others, miscellaneous, 1580–1682. Fair to very
good, 6 in brass.   14
800 Of cities. Artois (all brass), Louis XIV, do. XV, 4 Dijon
(all personal), 1616 to 1769. Good to fine.   19
801 Burgundy. 1648 to 1743. Only one with bust ; others are
mostly with arms on obv. Fair to v. good.   12
802 Nantes. 1653 to 1752. All with arms of the city ; some are
personal, with others miscellaneous, 1542 to 1699. Mostly
good to fine.   12
803 Duplicates of the French series, includes coins, jetons, etc.
Many good.   54
804 Another lot, in quality and kind quite as last.   55

SPAIN.

805 Ferdinand and Isabel. Octavo, Quarto and double Quarto.
F & Y. and castle. ℞ Lion. (2 of latter, and varying).
Very fair and very good. 18, 25, 30.   3
806 Octavos (2 varying and unlike the preceding) and dbl Quarto,
differing. Good to about fine. Phil. II, 2 M. Fair ; per-
haps found no better.   4
807 Phil. III. 2, 4 and 8 Maravedis, 1598–1619. Mostly good ;
6 CS. changing values to VI, 8 and XII.   13
808 1612 8 Mar., Segovia mint. Castle. ℞ Lion, each in shield.
Fine and rare ; on square planchet. 30 x 31.   1
809 Phil. IV. 1621 8 Mar. as last ; also 1624 CS. 1642 and XII,
and another of same date, CS. XII ; new type 1628, R X
cwnd. ℞ Monogram. 1 and 4 Mar. Bust *r*. ℞ VIII | s
bet. pillars, cwnd. Thick ; a rare var. but coarse work.   6
810 Various. III, VI, 8 (and VIII) and XII Maravedis, all CS.
and from a number of mints. Some are twice dated ; others
have 2 values, confusion probably averted by date ; generally
wretched work.   24
811 Another asst., selected to be an equal of the preceding.   25
812 Phil. V. 8 and 16 Maravedis, 1661–64. All with bust ; a var.
of mints and marks ; some dated on obv. Mostly good to
fine.   18

b 813 Chas. II, 2 Mar., 1680, '84, '85. Phil. V, 3, 4 and 6 Mar.,
        etc., 1708–11. Good to fine ; 2 are rare.   9

c 814 Phil. V, 1, 2 and 4 Mar., 1718–46. Lion and globes. Also 1
        Mar., Ferd. VI, 1746, same type, and a small coin with P.
        cwnd. ℞ Lion in shield. Mostly very good.   15

815 Chas. III. Bust *r.* ℞ Arms within wreath. 1, 2, 4 and 8
        Mar., 1772–88. Mostly choice, some in mint state. Very
        desirable.   35

c 816 Chas. IV. Type and values as last (but one of the 1 Mar.),
        1788–1808. Mostly good to unc. ; some red or partly so.   27

817 Jos. Napoleon. Bust *l.* sep. 8 — M. 8 Mar., 1810, '11, '12,
        '13. Very fair to good ; rare, and, I believe, a complete set
        of dates of his copper coins.   4

818 Ferd. VII. Bare head *r.* J. mint. 1814 4 Mar., rare ; 8 do.
        1812–17. Good to fine.   7

819 Laur. head. Same mint. 2 Mar., 1818, '19, '20 ; 4 do., 1819,
        '20, all rare ; 8 do., 1818–21. One fair, others good to
        fine.   9

820 Segovia mint (m. m. an aqueduct). Laur. head *r.* 2 Mar.,
        1817–33 (11) ; 4 do., 1824–33 (8) ; 8 do., 1816–33 (7).
        Dates prior to 1824 of this coinage are very rare. Mostly
        good to fine ; 1 holed ; 5 are in mint state.   26

c 821 Bare head *r.* Fern. 7° 8 Mar., 1822–23 ; Ferdin. VII, 2 Mar.,
        1824–26 ; 4 do., same dates ; 8 do., 1823–27. One Segovia
        mint, remainder Juba. One poor, others chiefly good to
        fine ; some rare.   12

822 Isabel II. 1 Mar., 1841 ; 2 do., 1838–58 (4) ; 4 do., 1837–55
        (13) ; 8 do., 1836 (value on rev.) to 55. Mostly good to
        unc. 10 of the last-named grade.   36

823 Cwnd arms. ℞ Value within circle. 1848 Medio Real, Ma-
        drid mint. 1850 Sim. type, a small wreath added above
        value, Decima and Medio. 1851 Medio. 1852 Decima
        and Medio. 1853 Decima and Dbl Decima. All Segovia
        mint, and rare ; 1 fair, others unc., 5 partly bright.   8

c 824 Head *r.* 10c. de Real, 1855–62 (7) ; 25c. de R., 1855–64 (8).
        Head *r.*, hair in heavy coil, curl on neck. ½, 1, 2½ and 5c.
        de Escudo. Good, some fine.   23

825 Republic. 1870 1, 2, 5 and 10 Ctmos. Unc. Alphonso XII,
        1877, '78, '79, 5 and 10 Ctmos. Fine to unc.   10

826 Amadeus. 1871 Head *r.* ℞ Arms on mantle draped from
crown ; below, 25 Pesetas. Edge with raised letters. From
dies for a gold coin. About unc. ; partly bright.   1

827 Chas. VII, Pretender. 1875 Laureated head *r.* 5 and 10
Ctmos. Fine, 1 partly bright.   2

828 Duplicates and varieties. Ferd. and Is. (and 5 earlier that
are in base metal), Chas. and Joanna, Phil. III, IV, Chas.
II, Phil. V, Chas. III. Many fair to good, 1 holed.   45

829 Others : Chas. IV, Jos. Nap., Ferd. VII, Is. II, Rep., and
Alf. XII. Many good ; some very fine to unc.   47

830 **Provinces and Cities in Spain.** Barcelona. Phil. IV,
Louis XIII, XIV, and Phil. V, 1626 to 1708 ; Ardite and
Seiseno. Fair to very good. All uncommon.   11

831 French occupation. ½ (holed), 1, 2 and 4 Quartos, 1808 to
1812. Fine. The 3 smallest values are very uncommon.   4

832 Others of the same series. 2 Quartos, 1809 ; 4 do., 1808 to
1814, consecutive ; Ferd. VII, 1823, 3 and 6 Qtos. Good
to fine.   10

833 Balearic Isles. 1812 12 Dinero. Catalonia. Ferd. VI, 1755,
'56. Ardite. Ferd. VII, Octavo, Qto. and Medio, II, III,
and VI Qto., 1810 to '14. Mostly very good ; a scarce and
desirable lot.   13

834 Cataluna. Is. II, 2 Cuartos, 1836, '37, '38, '40, '41, '46 ; 6 do.
1836 to '39, '41, '43 to '46. Good to fine.   15

835 Ivica. Phil. IV, n. d., Chas. II, 1686 Sueldo, and 2 smaller
pieces that do not show date. A very crude and imperfect
coinage. Rare. 21, 24, 26. Majorca. Chas. II, Phil. V,
and Louis I, 1, 2 and 6 Dinero. Poor and fair.   8

836 Majorca. FERDIN. VII. D. G. ETC. HISP. REX. 1823 8 Maravedis. Laur. head *r.* sep. P — 8, otherwise type of Segovia
and other mints of the period. A very fine, original, and
extremely rare cast for Palma. 28.   1

837 Navarre. Phil. IV, V, Cuartos and 2 Mar., 1718, (only date
shown). Ferd. III (VII of Spain), 1826, 1 and 3 Mar., date
on obv. ; 1830, same values, date on rev. ; 1832, ½ Mar.,
Arms. 13 x 13. Poor to very good ; all rare.   11

838 — 1820 1, 3 and 6 Maravedis. Laur. head *r.*, sep. value. ℞
Arms on cross, depending from crown, P — P. Good, very
rare. 18, 25, 33.   3

/: 839 Pampeluna. Is. II, 1837 8 Mar. Type of her first coinage,
with 8 PP M. below arms on rev. A fair, original brass
cast, very rare. Perpignan, 1648 ; Larida, very early (2) ;
Tarragona, a large T., a coin of uncertain city in Catalonia.
A — ? sep. castle in frame. Fair to very good ; a rare lot.   6

/ 840 Duplicates. A variety of provinces and cities. Includes Catalonia, Ivica (6 of the largest kind, 2 show date), Majorca,
Navarre and Tarragona. Poor to fine ; rare.   23

PORTUGAL.

t 841 1384–1521, John I, Eduardus, Alphonsus (V), John II and
Emanuel. Poor to good.   16

2 842 Others of same period. Poor and fair, 1 holed.   13

// 843 John III, 3 Reals, fair ; X, do., fine but holed ; Sebastian,
Real and 3 Reals (2, one with L — 3 for Lisbon), also 5 do.
with large V on rev. Good ; a rare lot. 21 to 39.   6

/ 844 John IV, 1½ (2 var.) and V Reis ; Peter II, 1677, 3, V and X
do. (The V is without date). Poor to nearly good ; all rare.
26 to 38.   7

/ 845 Peter II, 1688, 1½ Reis. Arms. ℟ Value within quatre-foil ;
others with P II cwnd. 1699, 1½, III, V and X Reis. 1703,
1½, III and V do. One fair, others good to fine. 22 to 36. 8

/ 846 John V. J. V crowned. 1713, V and X Reis. 1714, 1½, III
do. 1720, III, X do. 1721, X do. Mostly good to fine.
27 to 37.   8

/ 847 Crowned arms. Varying dates of III (5), V (8) and X (13)
Reis, 1723 to '49. Poor to fine ; average v. good.   26

848 Jos. I. Varying dates of III, V (6) and X (8) Reis, 1752–76.
Mostly very good.   15

/ 849 Maria I and Peter III. III, V (4) and X (3) Reis, 1777–85.
Maria I. III, V (3) and X (4) do., 1791–1812. Many fine.   16

/ 850 John, Prince Regent. III, V and X Reis, 1804–13 (5) ; 40
do. with bust, 1811–15, consecutive. Good to fine.   10

851 John VI. V and X Reis, arms, and 40 do. with bust, 1819–25
consecutive. Good ; a few fine.   9

/ 852 1820 Pattern 10 Reis. DECVS ET TVTAMEN Cwnd arms. ℟
TVETVR ET ORNAT Within wreath X, date below. Unc.,
partly bright. Very rare. 34.   1

853 Peter IV. 40 Reis, 1826, '27, '28, with bust. Michael I.
V Reis, 1829 ; X do., 1829, '31 ; 40 do., 1828–30 consecutive. Arms only. Good to fine. 12

854 Maria II. V, X, XX and 40 Reis, 1830 to '53, representing
four coinages, including a X Reis of 1836 in lead ; probably
a pattern. Many fine, some unc., red. 35

855 1833 40 Reis. Arms, similar to those displayed on the common thick piece, but top of arms shield is pointed at sides.
Probably a pattern. Unc. Brass. Very rare. 34. 1

856 1833 Another of same design, differently executed. Fine ;
planchet slightly defective, size 38. Also a much-worn 40
Reis of 1847, CS. G.(overno) C.(ivil) P.(orto.) Rare. 2

857 Louis I. III (2), V (8), X (2) and XX Reis. Arms type,
1867–79. V (4), X (4) and XX (3) do. Bust type, 1882–86.
Mostly good to fine, some unc. 26

858 Jos. I. 1772 In copper and brass, and Maria I and Peter III,
1781. Patterns for gold coins, from Rio mint. Unc. 33. 3

859 Duplicates and varieties of Portuguese coins. John I, III,
Sebastian, Peter II, John V, Jos. I, Maria I, and Peter III.
Poor to fine ; contains some desirable pcs. 34

860 Others : John, P. R., to Louis I. Many large ; mostly good
to fine. 35

861 **Gibraltar.** 1802, Keeling's ; 1810, same firm ; 1813, Cat-
ton's ; 1820, Spittle's, 1 and 2 Quartos of each. 1842, Victoria, ½, 1 and 2 do. Good to fine ; none common, some
rare. 11

RUSSIA.

862 Alex. Michaelowicz. 1645–76, 1 Kopeck. The Czar mtd.
2 var., very good. Oblong, 8 x 12. Also *restrikes* of the
extremely rare 2 and 3 Kopecks of same type. Very fine. 4

863 Peter the Great. ¼ Kopeck, 3 var. ; ½ do., 2 var. ; 1 do., 2
var., and 5 do. ¼ dated 1722, the 5 K. 1723 ; remainder
have Russian figures. Also a Beard Token, 1705 (in Russian), nose, moustache and chin whiskers, CS. with dbl-hd
eagle. Good to fine ; a lot of rare pieces. 13 to 28. 9

864 Varieties and differing years (all but 5 in Russian). ¼ Kopeck
(10, 3 var., 2 sizes), ½ do. (2), 1 do. (3). Very good. 16

865 Another lot, similarly asstd. and varying. Good and v. good. 16

866 Others : ½ Kopeck (4), 1 do. (16). Dates all in Russian. The 1 Kopeck (and all preceding) have St. George killing the dragon. Good to fine.   20

867 1725 5 Kopecks. Arms and 5 dots. ℞ Value and date in cross form. 33½. Proof ; probably a *restrike.*   1

868 Catharine I. 1726 Kopeck. Arms within dotted circle, date in angles, 1-7-2-6. ℞ Blank. V. good, v. rare. 25 x 25.   1

869 1726 5 Kopecks, similar. Arms sep. date, 17–26. V. fine ; probably a *restrike.* 42 x 43.   1

870 1726 10 Kopecks. Arms within dotted circle in the 4 corners, in centre, value, date, etc. ℞ Blank. A *restrike.* V. fine. 62 x 62.   1

871 1726, '27, 5 Kopecks. Peter II, 1728 (2 die var.), '29, Moscow Kopecks, with St. George. 1729, '30, 5 Kopecks. Good to fine.   7

872 1728 Moscow Kopeck. *Restrike,* proof.   1

873 ¼ and ½ Kopecks of Anna, John III and Elizabeth I, 1730–54. Arms. ℞ Value and date in cartouche. Others of Eliz., 1755, 1 Kopeck. Eagle on clouds (uncirculated). 1757, ¼, ½, 1 and 2 Kopecks. St. George. ℞ Monogram. 1761, 5 do. Arms. ℞ Mon. Fair to fine.   12

874 Differing dates of ¼ and ½ Kopecks, as first mentioned in last lot. Good to fine.   34

875 Elizabeth. 5 Kopecks. Eagle on clouds. 1755 (2), '56 (3), '57, dif. moneyers, plain and lettered edges. Very good.   6

876 Varieties and differing dates, of type with monogram on rev. ¼, ½ (2), 1 (2), 2 (6) and 5 (3) Kopecks, 1758-60. Fair to very good.   14

877 Another lot, still varying. ½, 1 (2), 2 (5) and 5 (4) Kopecks. Fair to very good.   12

878 1757 ¼, ½, 1 and 2 Kopecks, St. George type, and 5 do. dbl-headed eagle. Patterns. *Restrikes.* Unc., red. Rare.   5

879 1761 ½, 2, 4 and 10 Kopecks. Dbl-hd. eagle. ℞ Value and date in 4 lines ; above, drum, flag, cannon, etc. Proof patterns. *Restrikes.* Rare. 23, 30, 38, 48.   4

880 Peter III. 1762 2, 4 and 10 Kopecks, type as last. Very good to about fine ; rare.   3

881 1762 Varieties of last. 2, 4 (2) and 10 (2) Kopecks. Fair to about fine ; rare.   5

882 Cath. II. 1765 ¼, ½, 1 and 2 Kopecks, St. George type, and 5 do. dbl-hd. eagle. The last is from Ekaterinburg mint; the others are without mint mark. Proof patterns. The first three are probably *restrikes.* Very rare.   5

883 1765 5 Kopecks from Ekaterinburg mint, and from a dif. die from that in preceding lot. A bronzed proof ; very rare.   1

884 ¼, ½, 1, 2 and 5 Kopecks, 1771–96. All E. mint, and fine.   5

885 5 Kopecks, 1783, '84, '85, '86, Kolywan mint. Uncirculated, *bright red.* Extremely rare when in such perfect preservation. Large coins size 44.   4

886 5 Kopecks, precisely as last. 1787, '91, '92, '95, '96.   5

887 Various mints and die varieties, 1763–73. ¼ (6), ½ (9), 1 (3), 2 (12) and 5 (8) Kopecks. Many good ; some fine.   38

888 Another ass't, 1767–90. Varied and quite as good.   40

889 Another, 1777–96, the equal of either of the two preceding.   45

890 Varieties of mints, etc., of the 10 Kopeck, 1763–82. Mostly good.   12

891 Others, 1786–90. Mostly very good, some fine.   12

892 Others, 1790–93. Mostly fine.   10

893 Others, 1793–96. Fine.   10

894 1771 Pattern Rouble. Date in shield on dbl-head eagle within ₁₀ banded wreath. ℞ MONETA | RUBLE (in Russian), both in depressions, 38 mlm. Edge lettered in script capitals. V. fine ; thickness of planchet 26, breadth 75.   1

A *restrike* of 1836, with newly-engraved edge ; determined by the inscription, which is divided into three portions instead of four, as on the original. The whereabouts of the original is believed to be unknown to-day, and these restrikes are very rare.

895 1796 Pattern set. E. II, cwnd. Dots around border indicate value. ¼, ½, 1, 2 (2 var. of edge), 4, 5 and 10 Kopecks. Plain edges excepting the 1 and 2 K. Very choice ; all partly bright. 16 to 45.   8

896 1796 Another set of sim. design, and from dies differing but slightly. ¼, ½, 1, 2, 4, 5 and 10 Kopecks. Edges diagonally milled ; all but first and last are proofs.   7

897 Paul I. 1797 ¼, ½, 1 and 2 Kopecks. The ¼ and ½ E. M. ; the others without *m.m.* Edges diagonally milled. Proofs ; very rare.   4

898 1797 ¼, ½ Kopeck ; 1800 ¼ do. ; 1801 ½ and 2 do. All (K. M.)
     Kolywan mint. Unc., the 2 K. bright red.   5
899 1797 ¼, ½, 1 and 2 Kopecks, Annenskoie mint (A. M.) ; also
     same values from Ekaterinburg mint (E. M.), dates 1798 to
     1801. Fine.   8
900 Various mints and dates of ¼ (2), ½ (5), 1 (4) and 2 (10) Kop.
     1797–1800. Good to fine.   21
901 Alex. I.   1802 ½, 1, 2 and 5 Kopecks, Ekaterinburg mint ; the
     last 3 struck as proofs. Rare.   4
902 Others of same mint, ¼, ½, 1, 2 and 5 Kopecks, 1803–05. Gd.
     to fine.   5
903 Others, ¼ (2), 2 and 5 (3) Kopecks, 1803–10. Good.   6
904 Others, 5 Kopecks, 1806, '07, '08, '09, '10. Fine.   5
905 Kolywan mint (m.m. on obv.), ¼, ½ and 1 Kopeck, all unc.,
     and 5 do. fine, 1802–09.   4
906 Others, ¼, ½ Kopeck, 1804 ; 1 do. 1805 ; 5 do. 1802, '03, '05.
     Good to fine, 1 unc.   6
907 Others, ¼ Kopeck, 1807, '10 ; 1 do. 1805, '07, and 5 do. 1804,
     '06, '07, '09. Good to unc.   8
908 *Second Coinage.* Dbl-hd eagle and date. ℞ Value in wreath.
     1810 ½, 1 and 2 Kopecks ; 1811 1 do., St. Petersburg mint ;
     1810 ½, 1 and 2 Kopecks, Ekaterinburg mint. Proofs, and
     rare.   7
909 Various mints and moneyers. ½ Kopeck, 1810, '11 (3) ; 1 do.
     1812–20 (6) ; 2 do. 1810–20 (consecutive, 15). Gd. to fine ;
     a few unc.   24
910 Others, differing. ½ Kopeck, 1812–14 (3) ; 1 do. 1811–23 (8) ;
     2 do. 1810–20 (consecutive, 14). Good to fine.   25
911 Others, still varying. ½ Kopeck, 1814–19 (4) ; 1 do. 1811–25
     (9) ; 2 do., 1810–14 (consecutive, 8). Good to fine.   21
912 Others, 2 Kopecks, 1817, '18, '21 to 25. Good to fine.   15
913 Nicholas I. ½ Kopeck, 1827, '28 ; 1 do. 1827 to 30 (5) ; 2 do.
     1826 to '29 (6). Various mints and moneyers, same type
     as last described. Good to unc., red.   13
914 *Second Coinage.* 1831 1, 2, 5 and 10 Kopecks. Unc., mostly
     red.   4
915 1834 Another set as last in every respect.   4
916 1839 Another, all bright red.   4

917 Another set, 1 Kopeck, 1836; 2 do. 1832; 5 and 10 do. 1837.
Bright red. 4

918 Others, 5 Kopecks, 1832, '33, '37, '38, and 10 do. 1838. Unc.
3 bright red. 5

919 Others, 1 Kopeck, 1832, '33, '34; 2 do. 1830, '37, '38; 5 do.
1831, '32, '33; 10 do., 1832, '33, '34. Good to unc. 12

920 Others, varying dates (1833–37) and moneyers. 1 Kopeck
(5), 5 do. (4), 10 do. (6). Mostly very good. 15

921 *Third Coinage.* The script Russian N, crowned. 1840 ¼, ½,
1, 2 and 3 Kopecks. Proofs, from the Ekaterinburg mint.
Rare. 5

922 St. Petersburg mint. ¼ and ½ Kopeck, 1840, '41, '42; 1, 2 and
3 do. 1840, '41, '42, '43. Good to very fine. 18

923 Suzun mint (C. M.) ¼ Kopeck, 1840, '41; ½ do. 1841 to '45;
1 do. 1840, '42, '43; 3 do. 1840, '45, '47. Good to fine.
Warsaw mint (M. W.) ¼ Kopeck, 1848. Unc. 15

924 Ekaterinburg mint (E. M.) ¼ Kopeck, 1841; ½ and 1 do.
1840 to '43; 2 do. 1841 to '44; 3 do. 1840 to '44. Good to
very fine. 19

925 *Fourth Coinage.* 1854 ¼ and ½ Kopeck. The Russian letter
N, crowned. 2, 3 and 5 do. Arms. ℞ Value and date.
Proofs, from E. mint; a little dull. 5

926 Ekaterinburg mint. ¼ Kopeck, 1850, '51, '52; ½ do. 1850 to
'53; 1 do. 1850 to '55; 2 and 3 do. 1850 to '55, excepting 2
K. 1854; 5 do. 1850, '51, '52. Mostly v. good; a few unc. 26

927 With B(anco) M(oneta,) Warsaw. ½ and 1 Kopeck, 1850–53,
'55; 2 do. 1851, '55; 3 do. 1850, '51, '52, '54; 5 do. 1850–53.
Good to unc. 20

928 Alex. II. 1856 ¼ Kopeck, unc.; ½, 1, 2, 3 and 5 do. Proofs,
from E. mint. 6

929 Others of same mint, differing dates, 1855–67. ¼ Kopeck (6),
½ do. (8), 1 do. (11), 2 do. (10), 3 do. (9), 5 do. (10). Good
to fine. 54

930 For Warsaw. 1855–64 ½ Kopecks (7), 1 do. (8), 2 do. (3), 3
do. (5). Good to fine. 23

931 *Second Coinage.* 1867–81 Date incuse on border (on 1 to 5
Kop.); all have milled edge; St. P. mint. ¼ Kopeck (4), ½
do. (8), 1 do. (10), 2 do. (9), 3 do. (8), 5 do. (8). Mostly
fine to unc. 47

932 E. mint. 1867–76 ¼ Kopeck (4), ½ do., 1 do. (7), 2 do. (7), 3
     do. (7), 5 do. (9). With few exceptions, fine to unc.   35

933 Alex. III. 1882 ¼, ½, 1, 2 and 3 Kop.; type same as last in
     preceding reign, St. P. mint. Proofs; obvs. not brilliant.   5

934 Others, 1882–86 ¼ Kopeck (2), ½ do. (2), 1 do. (3), 2 do., 3 do.
     (3). Many unc.   11

935 **Unassorted Duplicates** of Russian coins from Peter the
     Great, 1724, to Alex. III, 1882. ¼ to 5 Kopecks. 21 of last
     century; none of Cath. II, and but 1 of Eliz., a 5 Kop., 1755.
     Unc., red; many good to fine.   55

936 Others, chiefly Canadian and late English shop cards, in brass,
     some very large. Good to fine make up the majority.   103

937 England. Wm. and Mary, and Wm. alone, Halfpennies, both
     very good. Isle of Man, 1709–1839 (11), Gibraltar, etc.,
     including Nuremberg, Jetons of Chas. and Cath. and Geo.
     II. Fair to fine.   21

938 — Tokens of the 19th century, chiefly 1811–15. Halfpennies,
     22; Pennies, 27. Many good, some fine.   49

939 — Birmingham. Threepence, 1813, nearly fine, some nicks.
     Norwich, Twopence, about good.   2

940 Holland. Jetons, 16th and 17th centuries. Fair to fine.   40

941 Another lot in same condition.   55

942 Another, and as good as either of the preceding.   73

943 Scandinavia and Low Countries, many early, including the
     square 8 Skilling pc. of Chris. V, same as described in lot
     736. In very fair condition. Fair to fine.   71

944 The poor and holed. This lot is more varied in character than
     any I have before culled from a collection. There are some
     scarce pcs., and a large number are early dated.   321

SIEGE AND NECESSITY PIECES.

Since the greater portion of the pieces arranged under this heading are rare,
it has been deemed best to avoid the constant repetition of the word.

Æ, Silver. Æ, Copper.

945 Aire. Besieged by the Allies, 1710. 25 Sols. Arms on cir-
     cular disc, cwnd. Good. Æ 22 x 24.   1

946 Amsterdam. Besieged and taken by troops of the States of
     Holland, 1578. V and X Sols. Arms of the city, cwnd,
     sep. date and value. Gd. and fine. Æ 18 x 18 and 24 x 24.   2

947 Amsterdam. 1578 X Sols. Same type, with rev. P | AR. ET |
 PO within closed and banded wreath. Good. ℝ 34 x 35. 1
948 — 1578 Sim. design for XL Sols. Arms support date, value
 below. ℞ As last. Obv. slightly dbl struck, otherwise fine.
 ℝ 37 x 38. 1
949 — 1578 V Sols. Arms cwnd, value and date in depression
 below, in two lines, CS. with a pedestal. (?) Fine. ℝ
 21 x 22. 1
950 — 1578 XL Sols. Same design; small CS., Brabant cross.
 Fine. ℝ 38 x 38. 1
951 — 1578 XL Sols, similar, CS. P. S. linked. Fine. ℝ
 38 x 40. 1
952 Antwerp. 1814 5 and 10 Ctms. 3 die varieties of each, N.
 for Napoleon within wreath, ANVERS above. Also 4 die var.
 of 10 Ctms. by Louis XVIII, 2 script L's linked. Good to
 fine. Æ 29 to 34. 10
953 Braunau. 1743 1, 3 and 30 Krzrs. Cwnd arms, revs. plain.
 Octagonal, 12, 16, 28. Good to fine. Lead. 3
954 Breda. Besieged by the Spaniards, 1625. 1 Sol, city arms
 sep. value; 2 do., BREDA OBSESSA Arms sep. date. Fine.
 Æ 13 x 14 and 18 x 18. 2
955 — 1625 20 Sols. Sim. design, value CS., also a rose. Fine.
 ℝ 20 x 21. 1
956 — 1625 40 Sols. Sim. design, different arms, CS. value, rose
 and city arms. Fine. ℝ 30 x 30. 1
957 Brussels. Beleaguered by the Spaniards, 1579. 18 Stuivers
 City arms, 18 St. above, PERFER ET OBDVRA etc. ℞ Plain.
 Fine. ℝ 24 x 26. 1
958 — 1579 36 Stuivers, same design. Fine. ℝ 34 x 34. 1
959 Cambray. 1581 2 Petards. Arms, town name and date CS.
 within beaded circle, sep. II—P as CS. Neumann, 37048.
 Good. Æ 24. 1
959a — Besieged by the Spaniards, 1595. Henry, Protector. HEN-
 RICO PROTECTORI in circle, within, 3 fleurs de lis. V — P.
 5 Petards. ℞ Plain. In parchment, leather, and lead. Van
 Loon, Vol. I, p. 458, No. 3. Fine. Octagon, 28. 3
960 Campen. Besieged and taken by the troops of the States,
 1578. 42 Stuivers. EXTREMVM | SVBSIDIVM etc. City arms.
 Very fine. ℝ 39 x 39. 1

961 Cyprus. 1570 Bisante. Good ; part of date dbl struck. Æ, 28. Daventer. Blockaded by the troops of the States, 1578. ½, 1, 2 and 4 Sols. Eagle, rev. value, all CS. with city arms. Good to fine. Æ 22 to 32.   5

962 Groningen. 1577 25 Stuivers. NECESSITATE 4 FEB City arms. Made from silver ware left by the Spaniards to pay their soldiers. Fine. Æ 30 x 31.   1

963 — 1672 Besieged without success by the Bishops of Munster and Cologne. 6 and 12 Stuivers. Cwnd arms sep. value. IVRE ET TEMPORE Fine. Æ 19 x 21 and 24 x 24.   2

964 — 1672 25 Stuivers, same design. Fine. Æ 27 x 28.   1

965 — 1672 50 Stuivers, same design. Very fine. Æ 35 x 36.   1

966 — 1672 50 Stuivers, sim. to last ; design enlarged to 31 mlm. Very fine. Æ 35 x 35.   1

967 Haarlem. Besieged and taken by the Spaniards, 1572. 15 Stuivers. Perpendicular sword, surmounted by cross, bet. 4 stars, CS. Lion and 3 stars. Very fine. Æ 25 x 26.   1

968 — 1572 30 Stvrs. Same design, CS. a star and crescent, also lion. Good. Æ 32 x 35.   1

969 — 1572 30 Stvrs. Similar, CS. a cluster of 3 stars. Fine. Æ 34 x 34.   1

970 — 1573 30 Stvrs. Arms on shield sep. date. CS. a star and crescent. Fine. Æ 32 x 33.   1

971 Julich. Fred. Pythian, Gov. 1621 2 Sols. F P. in mon. sep. date and value in 6 CS. around border. Fine. Æ Hepta-gon, 33.   1

972 Landau. Besieged by the French, 1713. 1 Florin, 4 Krzrs. Arms. C. A. in script mon., CS. in 4 corners. Fine ; loop removed. Æ 32 x 35.   1

973 — 1713 2 Florin, 8 Krzrs. of similar design. Fine ; loop removed. Æ Octagon, 38 x 45.   1

974 Leyden. 1573 ½ Stuiver. Fair. Æ 21. 1574 5 Sols. PVGNO PRO PATRIA Lion, etc. Good. Parchment. 30.   2

975 — 1574 Demi Daalder. Same type as the parchment pc. ℞ LVG | DVNVM | RVM Fine. Æ 31½.   1

976 Lille. 1708 X and XX Sols. Luxemburg besieged by the French, 1795. 1 Sol, an original brass cast. Mantua (1799) Soldo, also a cast as last. Good to fine.   4

977 Maestricht. Besieged by the Spaniards under the Duke of
Parma, 1579. I, II (both holed), VIII, XVI, XXIIII and
XXXX Sols. Arms (a star) in shield, surmounted by erect
sword, sep. date and inscription. Good to fine. Æ 24 to
39½. 6

978 Mayence. Besieged by the French, 1793. 1 (2 die var.), 2
(2) and 5 Sols. Fasces bet. branches crossed. Palma
Nuova. 1814 50 Ctmi. NAPOLEONE IMPE etc. Good to
fine. Æ 21 to 35. 5

979 Middleburg. Besieged by the Zeelanders, 1572. 25 Stuivers.
D. R. P. | F. MIDD | 1 · 5 · 7 · 2 CS. with arms of Zeeland
and Tournay, both small. Very fine. Ꞧ 29½ x 31. 1

980 — 1572 50 Stuivers, same design. V. fine. Ꞧ 33 x 36. 1

981 Roman Republic. 1849 V, X, XX and XL Baiocchi. Rom-
ulus and Remus suckled by wolf; not official pieces, only
speculative issues. Very fine. Brass, silvered. 14 x 14 to
32 x 32. 4

982 Schoonhaven. VI | S 6 Stvrs. ℞ Incuse of obv. Good. Æ
22. Tournay. Besieged by the Allies, 1709. 2 and 8 Sols,
dif. arms. Good. Æ 24, 29. 3

983 Tournay. (1707) 20 Sols. Bust of DE SVRVILLE /. Good.
Ꞧ 20 x 21. 1

984 Ulm. 1704 City arms. ℞ Imperial arms. Good. Ꞧ 30 x 30. 1

985 Utrecht. 1707 3 Petards. 3 — P. Arms, date below. Brass,
25 x 25. Zamoscia. 1813 6 Groszy. Æ 33. Both v. good. 2

986 Westphalia. Munster. Besieged by its own Bishop, 1666.
Thaler. Arms of Munster. Fine. Ꞧ 32 x 32. 1

987 Wismar. 1-7-1-5 stamped in the 4 corners. In field, within
circle, 8 | SCHILL * | WISM ⁂ All incuse. ℞ Plain. Plan-
chet ⁷⁄₈ in. thick. Very good. Æ 60 x 63. 1

988 Zeeland. 1574 · I · 5 · | LIBERT : | REST : S. P. Q. ZEL · | · SOLI ·
DEO | · HONOR · | · 7 · 4 · within beaded circle, arms of Zee-
land CS. above. Good. Ꞧ 29 x 30. 1

989 — 1574 Another, similarly inscribed, with date 1 · 5 · 7 · 4
in first line, a sprig above and below. Fine. Ꞧ 36 x 36. 1

990 Zierikzee. Besieged by the Spaniards, 1576. Daalder or 100
Sols. + REGIÆ | MAT RECON | etc. in 6 lines. Fine. Ꞧ
36 x 36. 1

Black Walnut Coin Cabinets

In good order, with locks and keys. Dimensions of drawers are inside measurements.

991 Length 38½ in., breadth 19 in., height 38 in., including 44 velvet-lined drawers in two tiers, 16 x 15 in. area and ⅜ in. deep; double doors, and a base with large drawer for catalogues.

992 Length 38½ in., breadth 20 in., height 24½ in., with 44 drawers, 16 x 15⅞ in. and ⅜ in. deep; double doors.

993 Larger than either of the preceding; has 4 separate cabinets, 3 in one tier, and the fourth above the centre one, on a stand projecting 9½ inches in front. Height to top of tier of three, 35 in., length 44½, breadth 17½; contains 76 drawers, 13⅛ x 12³⁄₁₆ in., and ½ in. deep.

PHOTOGRAVURE PLATES.

11   27   37   38

40   50   64   66

70   71   78   84

87   98   109   171

173   189   203   223

227   252   256   340

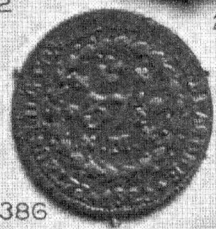

386

371   417   502

503   510   519

520   521   522

527   533   547

PLATE 2.

550 558 567 598

601 625 628 635

641 647 652 852

868 696 694

79

15

PLATE 3.

www.ingramcontent.com/pod-product-compliance
Lightning Source LLC
Chambersburg PA
CBHW031448270326
41930CB00007B/912